The Quest for Arthur

STUART McHARDY

Luath Press Limited

EDINBURGH

www.luath.co.uk

First Published 2001

The paper used in this book is recyclable. It is made from low
chlorine pulps produced in a low energy, low emission manner
from renewable forests.

Printed and bound by
Omnia Books Ltd., Glasgow

Typeset in Sabon by
S. Fairgrieve, Edinburgh 0131 658 1763

Map by Jim Lewis

To the memory of my father,
Jim McHardy

1919-1981

Acknowledgements

I would like to thank the City of Edinburgh Council Planning Department for the research and design grant they made available towards the completion of this book, and the volunteers and participants in the 1991 Festival of Myth, Legend and Folklore in Edinburgh, who stimulated my interest in Arthur.

Thanks to Tom Gray and the Tom and Sybil Gray Collection for the use of photographs of Vanora's Stone and the Aberlemno Kirkyard Stone. Thanks to Hugh McArthur for the use of his photographs of Dunadd, Dumbarton, the Corryvreckan and Ben Arthur. The photograph of Vanora's Mound was taken by my late friend Martin Henry.

Thanks also to Herbert Coutts, David Patterson and Bob McLean at Edinburgh City Art Centre, and to Helen Johnston.

Contents

Foreword

THIS BOOK COINCIDES WITH the exhibition *The Quest for Camelot* at Edinburgh City Art Centre which illustrates to a significant extent Stuart McHardy's thesis that Arthur is an historic figure who deserves to be given pride of place in the history of Scotland.

I have always believed that Edinburgh was Camelot. Even as a schoolboy, I knew there had to be evidence of Arthur in the history of Scotland. From the school playground in Portobello, I could see clearly the hill dominating the city centre skyline known as Arthur's Seat, instantly recognisable in the form of a 'Lion Couchant' and reminiscent of the Sphinx of Egypt. My youthful imagination populated that hill with Arthur and his Knights. Inspired by the poem 'The Lady of Shalott', I found myself illustrating many aspects of the Arthurian world conjured up in Tennyson's Victorian romanticism. Little did I realise then that Patrick Geddes had commissioned John Duncan to paint Arthur being rowed across Duddingston Loch by Merlin in the shadow of Arthur's Seat in search of Excalibur. The painting is one of a suite of murals in a room designed by Geddes to honour great figures in Scotland's history.

I am indebted to Stuart McHardy for writing the book that would have been invaluable to all the artists I invited to Scotland over the past four decades to consider the Arthurian dimension in the cultural heritage of Scotland, particularly through its bardic traditions. It should be required reading for artists and art teachers concerned with Scotland's cultural identity in 21st century Europe.

Professor Richard Demarco OBE
November 2001

Arthurian Locations in Scotland

1	Rhinns of Galloway	possible location of Arthurian fort
2	Loudon Hill/River Glen	probable site of Arthurian battle
3	Douglas	suggested site for series of Arthurian battles
4	Tinto Hill	ancient sacred fire site, not far from Merlin's well and cave on Hart Fell
5	Cademuir Hill	possible site of battle of Cat Coit Celidon
6	Eildon Hills	tradition of Arthur and his knights sleeping in hill
7	Stow	probable site of battle 'in castello Guinnion'
8	Traprain Law	major site of the Gododdin tribe
9	Isle of May	suggested site of Isle of Avalon
10	Edinburgh	probable location of battle of 'Mynyd Agned'
11	Bouden Hill	probable site of battle of Badon Hill
12	Falkirk	area with strong Arthurian traditions
13	Antonine Wall	Roman defensive structure
14	Dunipace	probable location of battle of 'Bassas'
15	Slamannan	placename associated with Gododdin tribe
16	Stirling	location of Kings' Knot
17	Dumyat	important fortified site of Maetae tribe
18	Clackmannan	placename associated with Gododdin tribe
19	Dollar	suggested site for Dolorous Gard
20	Dumbarton	site strongly associated with Arthur
21	Loch Lomond	one of Nennius's Wonders of Britain
22	Glen Douglas	possible site of series of Arthurian battles
23	Ben Arthur	mountain named after Arthur
24	Dunadd	capital of the Scots of Dalriada
25	Corryvreckan	the cauldron of the goddess - whirlpool
26	Meigle	site of Arthurian tale and Vanora's grave
27	Bennachie	ancient sacred hilltop site

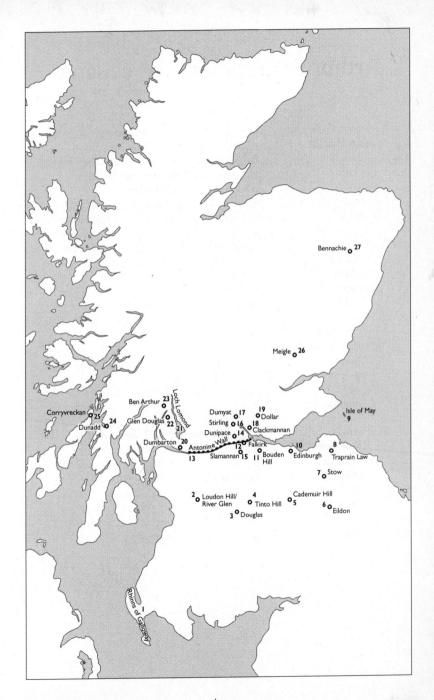

Bennachie 27

Meigle 26

Ben Arthur 23
Corryvreckan 25
Dunadd 24
Glen Douglas 22
21
Loch Lomond

Dumyat 17
Stirling 16
Dunipace 14
Dumbarton 20
Antonine Wall
13
Slamannan 15
Falkirk 12
Bouden Hill 11

19 Dollar
18 Clackmannan

Isle of May 9

Edinburgh 10
8 Traprain Law

7 Stow

2 Loudon Hill/
River Glen
3 Douglas

4 Tinto Hill 5

Cademuir Hill
6 Eildon

Rhinns of Galloway 1

ix

A page from the 13th century manuscript of the epic poem, *Y Gododdin*, probably composed by Aneurin c. 600 AD which includes the earliest literary reference to Arthur.

(Reproduced by kind permission of Cardiff City Libraries)

Introduction

ALTHOUGH THE FIGURE OF King Arthur is known throughout the world, it is little appreciated that the original stories about this great heroic figure seem to derive from that area of north Britain known since the ninth century as Scotland. Arthur is seen as a typical English or Welsh figure, while the scanty evidence of Arthur as a historical figure actually points to his northern origin. Just as the original mythological figure was that of a tribal hero, so the historic figure of the early sixth century was the leader of a war band rather than a king. The idea of the British king fighting off invaders from the Continent which is at the heart of most later developments of the Arthurian material is no longer sustainable in the light of modern scholarship. I put forward a different potential reason for Arthur's 12 battles.

Historians have long understood that the notion of the great feudal king with his Knights of the Round Table, the organised jousting tournaments and the romanticised notions of medieval chivalry are all creations of the early Middle Ages, but the notion of Arthur as coming from southern Britain persists. As early as the nineteenth century W. F. Skene put forward sites for the 12 battles of Arthur described by Nennius that could all be located in Scotland. Most commentators who have located the battles in England and Wales have had to suggest a wide geographical distribution, from Bath to Lincolnshire, from the Severn to the Scottish Borders. W. F. Skene suggested a series of locations that provides a basis for what can be seen as a concerted military campaign, and I have used his suggestions as the starting point for my analysis. I believe there are better potential sites for some of the battles than those suggested by W. F. Skene and I hope through my own ideas to move the argument forward and provide a starting point for further discussion.

Behind the figure of the romantic hero-king is a tribal warrior leader, and in such creations as the Round Table perhaps all we are seeing is a memory of a time when the warriors, like the rest of the family groups who made up the British tribes, sat around a central hearth to eat and to talk. However, strip away the romantic trappings of chivalry and idealised feudal kingship and even chivalry can be seen to echo the honour code of the tribal warrior – an honour code that respected the individual above all and in which no man could follow another he did not respect. In the ancient tales that contain the earliest Arthurian material we can see remnants of ancient pre-Christian beliefs, and in the women of these tales there are clear suggestions of a time when the role of the female was more significant than the later romances suggest. In the figure of Morgan we have a female closely related to goddess figures on the one hand, and on the other to a specific institution that existed within the pagan religion. In the stories of shape-changing that occur in several tales we have perhaps a remnant of beliefs that are linked to shamanistic practice, and in several tales from ancient Welsh sources we have references to beliefs that hark back to the very dawn of time.

Although we rely on Welsh sources for almost everything we know about the figure of Arthur, we should remember that the ancestor of Welsh, recently referred to as Common Archaic Neo-Brittonic, was spoken at one time, in one form or another, from Scotland down to northern France. And in Scotland it is now realised that the Picts, the people who lived in northern and eastern Scotland, spoke a similar P-Celtic language. Where languages are the same, or similar, it is likely that traditions and beliefs will likewise be very close. We rely today on history as a written discipline but it was not so for the people of sixth-century north Britain. They had only word of mouth and memory by which to learn and to pass on what they knew and considered important. Recent studies have shown the remarkable capacity of oral transmission to carry provable data over stunning periods of time – tens of thousands of years. Our reliance on the written word has blinded us to the value ancient tales can have. It is also true that even when written literature arrived in Britain, the old stories continued to be told amongst the people. Even today we have storytellers who have never learned to read or write yet who have vast treasuries of knowledge and lore that they carry with them wherever they go. As storytelling becomes more and more popular the value of such treasuries is better appreciated.

The stories of Arthur, of course, do not belong to Scottish culture – they are integral to Welsh, Cornish and Breton tradition and in literary terms Arthur is truly pan-European. Most people know of Thomas Malory's *Morte d'Arthur*, but are unaware of *Morte Arthur*, written at an earlier date by Sir Hugh of Eglintoun, a Scot. There are Arthurian romances like *Lancelot of the Laik, Golagros and Gawain* and *Sir Gawain and Sir Galeron of Galloway* which survive in the Scots language and various Arthurian tales that exist within Gaelic tradition. There are also motifs in many ancient Gaelic and Scots sources that echo the earliest Welsh sources we know of. Within these Welsh sources there are many references to both Pictish and Gaelic individuals, which is precisely what one would expect from material that originated in an area where the Britons, Picts and Scots co-existed. The only place this happened was in central Scotland. The peoples of the areas we know as Strathclyde and Manau Gododdin in the fifth and sixth centuries spoke Common Archaic Neo-Brittonic and their cousins the Picts spoke something similar. It is only in a later period that this language became restricted to Wales, leading to so much misinterpretation of British history. We now know that the influx of Germanic-speaking peoples from the Continent started much earlier, and lasted much longer, than earlier interpretations have suggested. The idea of the Anglo-Saxon invasion itself as a concerted campaign is no longer tenable. We also now know that language shifts do not occur only as a result of invasion and slaughter. To say that Arthur was a Welshman from Scotland shows the weakness of trying to def people by the language they speak, but as a tribal warrior speaking an earlier form of the Welsh language and living in Scotland, what can we call him?

The truth is that Arthur is now universal, a virtual archetype of the hero, and belongs to all of us. However, since the Treaty of Union in 1707 the realities of Scottish history have all too often been suppressed by the dictates of creating a British history in which the role of England has been dominant. This process has been as common amongst Scots, happy with the advantages of Empire, as amongst the English. Times change, empires fall and history itself is subject to being revisited. Many writers on Arthurian material have interpreted him as having been heavily influenced by the ideas of the Roman Empire. I suggest that by the early sixth century Roman influence, never greatly significant in Scotland, was essentially irrelevant. Furthermore, I believe that just as the earliest historians were influenced by their role as classically educated Christians, so many of our later historians have been over-influenced by a classical education that stressed the importance of Greece and Rome. This attitude has been further influenced by the fact that England was under Roman rule for centuries and so English history and culture has been greatly influenced by the Romans. And English history became British history. In Scotland this influence comes into play much later and is essentially restricted to the influence of classical education and in particular the long tradition of Latin scholarship that flourished in Scotland. On the ground in sixth-century Scotland the Romans were effectively irrelevant. The new religion, Christianity, that they brought with them was not.

Stuart McHardy
November 2001

Chapter One

Why, Where and When

IN JUNE 1991 I was the Assistant Director of the Festival of Myth, Legend and Folklore in Edinburgh. Over the course of the week-long event I met many people who were particularly interested in the ideas surrounding the romanticised figure of King Arthur. I had never paid much attention to Arthurian material, thinking of it as having nothing to do with the history and culture of my country, Scotland. In the course of that week however, talking to people about the provenance of the original Arthurian motifs, I began to think of this as an area worthy of study. I was already aware of significant areas of overlap in the traditional tales and legends of Scotland, Ireland, Wales and, to some extent, Scandinavia.

By the time I was in Australia in 1996 lecturing on a range of 'Celtic' topics at Melbourne's Centre for Adult Education I included a two-and-a-half-hour talk entitled 'Arthurian Connections in Scotland'. While there I went with my family and a friend to the top of a small hill called Arthur's Seat not far from Melbourne. There on the top of the hill was a giant metal chair with arms – an actual Arthur's seat. While this is an interesting and amusing visual joke it did make me think. Here was I on the far side of the world putting forward an idea that most of the students found revolutionary – that Arthur was extensively known in Scotland – and then coming across a typically ironic Australian reminder of what heroes can mean. The chair on Arthur's Seat stands over six feet high because after all wasn't Arthur a giant? In terms of being known across the planet there can be few legendary heroes that have made as much of a mark as him, that's for sure.

The figure of King Arthur is known all over the world, and not just in those places where the dominant language is English. The idea of the hero-king has inspired writers for 800 years in a variety of languages. Between 1200 and 1600 Arthurian traditions gave rise to stories or translations in Breton, Czech, Danish, Dutch, English, French, German, Greek, Hebrew, Icelandic, Italian, Old Norse, Portuguese, Provençal, Russian, Scots, Spanish, Swedish, and Yiddish. With the growth of the various European empires in the eighteenth and nineteenth centuries these stories became known worldwide. The nineteenth-century American writer and humorist Mark Twain wrote *A Yankee at King Arthur's Court* which in turn gave rise to a Hollywood film in 1949, the first of many to rework Arthurian traditions. Probably the best known of these is the film-musical *Camelot* (1967), based on a Broadway stage musical, though *Monty Python and the Holy Grail* (1975) is many people's favourite. In the majority of these works Arthur is presented as one of the world's great heroes in the guise of a medieval king, with his court full of chivalric knights dedicated to jousting and romantic love. He is also presented in many instances as the model of an English king, which given his real origins is more than a touch ironic.

The original historical Arthur was not a king but probably a temporary war leader, and in sixth-century Britain the men he led were far removed from the armoured knights of romance. Such institutions as jousting and the society of feudal knights were centuries in the future when Arthur was active in Britain. The great popularity of the theme of King Arthur has been said to have originally developed from Thomas Malory's *Morte d'Arthur* – one of the very first books published in Britain, by William Caxton in 1485 – and has been popular since then. Malory himself drew on a wide variety of medieval literature, in various languages, for his *magnum opus*, which was heavily influenced by Geoffrey of Monmouth's rather fanciful *The History of the Kings of Britain* written in the twelfth century. Before this printed publication there were many manuscripts of Arthurian romances in existence based in many cases on stories that were told all over Europe. The adoption of Arthurian material by storytellers, minstrels and, later, writers in so many different European societies was in fact an echo of ages-old storytelling traditions. By the Early Medieval period most of these stories were concerned with the adventures of a king and various hero-knight figures, but the origin of these tales lies much earlier than the Middle Ages.

Arguments have ranged for centuries over where the original Arthur stories were told and whether there was in fact an actual historical figure of that name in the sixth century. While it is impossible to answer these questions definitively, it is possible to assemble the evidence for Arthur's existence and his probable location and see if it makes a believable case to suggest a Scottish provenance. I believe much of the discussion to date on both the origin of the Arthurian stories and his own historicity has been substantially flawed. Just as the modern Hollywood version of Arthur and the Knights of the Round Table is based on a medieval reinterpretation of traditional material that originated, or at least survived, in the Welsh language, I believe most historians have misinterpreted the period of Dark Age Britain by imposing ideas and constructs from later societies. To try to understand who the original Arthur was it seems sensible to try to create as clear a picture of his contemporary society as we can. One of the problems to be faced at the very start of such an attempt is the fact that what early material we have comes from manuscripts written long after the sixth century. There are even scholars who see the works of the semi-mythical Welsh poet Taliesin as originating in the twelfth century with older references being little more than remnants of ancient traditions, included to give an air of authenticity. That great repository of ancient Welsh lore, *The Mabinogion*, survives in its current structure from original manuscripts no older than the fourteenth century, though some of the motifs and ideas contained in its tales are so old as to be virtually timeless. As to the historical sources that apply to the Arthurian period, they too are medieval copies of older works. What unites these different types of source material is that they are literature – they are written down.

History is a form of human communication dependant in the modern world on literature, and suffers from the same constraints as all literature. Literature is usually written by individuals and there are no individuals who are without cultural baggage. Think of the Second World War and then consider how it has been represented by the historians of the Soviet Union, the United Kingdom and the United States. Children in these different societies did not hear the same story. And when one considers how the period was represented in a popular medium such as film it is clear that 'history' is subject to all sorts of influences, and not always deliberately so. Just as Malory interpreted the Welsh tales as taking place in a feudal society akin to what he himself knew, so historians find it difficult to limit the effect of their own beliefs on what they write. I am no different, but I try. One of the points that arises time and again when we look at the earliest sources such as *The Mabinogion* is the clear masculine bias. However, when you look a little deeper it becomes obvious that things are not black and white as regards the relationship between the sexes and there are several powerful women in these tales. Later interpretations, however, do downplay the role of women, which goes some way to explaining why there is still much to discover in Arthurian traditions, as I hope to show.

Historians take pride in always comparing different source materials to come up with analyses but the further back we go the less literature there is. For some of the earliest records we will consider there are no others with which to compare them and they require considerable analysis. In Scottish terms there is very little early literature that has survived, and the extent to which the early Welsh sources can shine a light on early Scottish history is unappreciated. N. Chadwick in her article *Lost Literature of Celtic*

Scotland wrote: '[The] absence of written records of the British Church in Scotland is an unexplained puzzle but an important fact.' (p. 124) Actually, it is not unexplainable. Scotland has been subjected to various invasions from her southern neighbour at different periods in her history that have resulted in widespread destruction of early records, usually stolen from the abbeys and monasteries in which they were written. This happened when Edward 1 of England attempted to subjugate the country at the end of the thirteenth century and to a lesser extent when Oliver Cromwell invaded Scotland in the middle of the seventeenth century. In Edward's case he wanted to destroy or hide anything that showed his claim to overlordship of Scotland as having no historical standing whatsoever. In addition the Scots themselves did their bit to destroy their own history when the fanaticism of the Reformation led to an assault on all aspects of 'Popery' including much moveable church property, as well as buildings. Who knows what manuscripts were destroyed as part of this process?

The lack of such early records might make it seem an impossible task to look for Arthur in Dark Age north Britain – Scotland itself was hundreds of years in the future as were the nation states of Wales and England. However, there are other ways of interpreting the past than simply by reading early sources. We can access archaeological investigations, interpret a range of different literary creations and give greater consideration to material from the oral tradition, but all such sources should be approached critically. The earliest histories in the British Isles arose from annals kept by monasteries and abbeys. These were tables kept to calculate moveable dates such as Easter, and it became a habit of early scribes to put in noteworthy events alongside the entries for particular years. However, what was important to a Christian monk living inside a relatively closed community was not necessarily what the people then, or we today, would consider of primary importance. Other material that survives in early written forms comes from tales and stories passed by word of mouth that were written down by monks. When dealing with material that originated in the oral traditions of the indigenous people of these islands, material written by monks has to be treated circumspectly. In the sixth century Christianity was not the accepted religion throughout Britain and much pagan belief was inherent in the traditional material of people who were ostensibly members of the new faith. We should also remember that monks were trained in a system of education that derived specifically from classical Roman and Greek models. These models placed great importance on literacy, centralisation and hierarchic structures. In sixth-century Britain, even in those areas that had been under the rule of the Roman Empire, much of society was essentially tribal. In Scotland, Ireland and Wales tribalism was the norm. In Scottish terms tribal society continued into the middle of the eighteenth century before falling to the brutal power of centralised government, at Culloden, followed by extended episodes of what would now be called ethnic cleansing. There was a deliberate policy to destroy the last vestiges of Highland tribal society which had existed in one form or another since the Iron Age. That society, however, has much to teach us, as we shall see.

In sixth-century Scotland, while there is some evidence to suggest there may have been settlements of Germanic-speaking peoples for some hundreds of years, the majority of the population is thought to have been P-Celtic-speaking. Linguists have divided up the Celtic languages into P-Celtic and Q-Celtic. P-Celtic encompassed the languages of the British tribes from the south coast of England as far north as the Forth–Clyde axis and probably the Picts who lived in the north and east of Scotland at this time. Today P-Celtic survives amongst the Welsh and Breton peoples though there has been a recent scholarly revival in Cornish. Q-Celtic is the name given to the languages that survive today, if only just, in Irish and Scottish Gaelic. In the sixth century the peoples of Ireland, the Isle of Man, the Hebrides and much of Argyll in Scotland probably all spoke earlier forms of Q-Celtic. The languages are thought to have come from a common root in the distant past and at some stage long ago the P sound changed in some areas to a Q or hard C sound. An easy way of remembering this is to think of the Welshman Owen Map Owen in all likelihood having a Scottish or Irish cousin called Ewan Mac Ewan.

We can be relatively certain that in the sixth century both Gaelic (Q-Celtic) and British (P-Celtic) were being spoken in what we now call Scotland, with the possibility of some Germanic speakers in small settlements. The Romans had brought over troops recruited in the Low Countries of Europe and some of these would have settled at least in parts of England, including areas near Hadrian's Wall. This, combined with the contact that had been taking place for a considerable period over the North Sea, would strengthen the likelihood that some Germanic-speaking tribes might have settled in Scotland. There has long been debate as to whether the place name Dumfries refers to a settlement of Friesians – the North Sea was for a long time known as the Friesian Sea – or whether it is from the Gaelic *Dunphreas*, 'the fort of the thicket'. I would suggest that if 'the fort of the thicket' were a viable place name its components are so commonplace as to suggest there would be more than one instance of the name. One of the problems historians have faced in trying to gain a clear picture of what are still called the Dark Ages is that the idea of defining people as an ethnic group by the language they speak is a dubious process. I speak Scots and English today and am descended from people who spoke Scots and Gaelic and before that Gaelic and Pictish. My ethnicity is not defined by my language any more than is that of an Indian in Calcutta whose first language is English. A further complication is that people at the time would have seen themselves as belonging to a tribe, in which their family was rooted, not a nation or a state and certainly not to a culture defined by a language.

Today there is great flowering of interest in all things 'Celtic'. Properly speaking this is a term that should apply to language and art but has been applied to all sorts of human activity which supposedly arise from putative shared heritage in the far past, including music and even, recently, food! As Professor Simon James shows in *The Atlantic Celts*, the modern idea of a Celt would have been meaningless to any Gaelic or Welsh speaker before 1700. I see little sense in trying to define ethnicity by anything so dynamic and fluid as language, which, if it ever stops changing, soon dies. This modern fascination with all things 'Celtic' has unfortunate overtones of racism, when it seems clear from the archaeological record that there has been regular contact between and among peoples as far south as Africa since Megalithic times, which suggests that most of us are in fact mongrels in the racial sense, and are all the better for it. This is not to downgrade distinct cultures, merely to warn against an over-romanticisation of the past. In this respect it is well to remember the Roman writer Tacitus who described Germans as tall, big-boned, red-headed people, a description many people think of as being particularly 'Celtic'.

Because the Arthurian material survived in Welsh it has become an accepted fact that he must have originally been Welsh, or that the legendary material regarding him arose in Wales. However, an appreciation of how the stories told of him arose shows the weakness of this position. No one seriously doubts that the earliest reference to Arthur is contained in the poem *The Gododdin* (originally *Y Gododdin*), written in Scotland.

Other references to Arthur exist in the works attributed to the poet Taliesin, possibly originating in the Dark Ages, and the twelfth century Geoffrey of Monmouth's *The History of the Kings of Britain* and *Vita Merlini*. These works were themselves based on earlier oral traditions. The tribespeople of sixth-century Britain were illiterate, though at this time the expansion of Christianity

The Gododdin

This poem, surviving in Welsh, is believed to have been composed somewhere in southern Scotland in the seventh century and contains the earliest known reference to Arthur. It describes an ultimately tragic raid by a group of warriors from around Edinburgh to somewhere south called Catraeth. This has generally been interpreted as being Catterick in Yorkshire. For many years the poem was considered to be about a battle in some unknown, dynastic struggle, but recent scholarship leans towards it having been a raid gone wrong. Given the tribal background of north Britain at this time this seems highly likely. Some scholars think it was composed in the Strathclyde area and others have suggested it originated amongst the Picts. The title of the poem, *The Gododdin*, comes from the name of the people who inhabited the area from the Lothians in Scotland to the north of England and who were referred to by the Greek geographer Ptolemy in the second century AD as the Votadini. Their lands included Manau Gododdin, an area that perhaps encompassed the southern shores of the River Forth as far as Stirling, and perhaps some of the northern shores as well.

was spreading literacy at least among its own institutions. The term illiterate itself is of little help in understanding the true position; it simply means the inability to read and write. Societies in which oral transmission is the norm have what is called oral literature – vast stocks of traditional, practical, healing, agricultural and hunting lore which was passed on by word of mouth and practical example. In addition there were many stories which can be seen as primarily mythological and legendary which were used to pass on tribal culture. Mythology should be understood as the earliest form of religion in which the world and everything in it is explained, while legends deal with specific individuals, places and events. The passing on of such information to the children of the tribe is absolutely central to tribal existence and much of the moral precepts, historical awareness and sense of individual worth that were required in such societies would be passed on by this process. In order for this process to have maximum impact the stories that were first heard by the people as children would be set within their own physical environment. This gives an immediacy and a relevance that setting such material in some far off, never seen location could not have had. This process accounts for the widespread locations of specific storytelling motifs, not only within particular societies but within different societies and language groups. Specifically it shows why there are so many different Arthurian place names throughout the British Isles. Other types of material dealing with the magical and the supernatural would be set elsewhere, in the Underworld, on magical islands, though some recent interpretations see the possibility of historical events being recorded in what have long been thought to be purely mythological works.

While it is impossible to untangle exactly how such a system worked in the sixth century it is eminently practicable for a tribe that moved from one location to another to have carried their story-stock with them and to have taught their children from that corpus of tradition by placing the stories within the recognisable physical environment. These would not be the only stories told. We know that the peoples of Britain were great travellers as far back as the fourth millennium BC and early Mediterranean literary sources tell us that during the Roman period their seamanship was still considerable. People would travel to trade and would undoubtedly bring back stories, even if mainly for entertainment rather than education. Such stories might in time become part of the stock of stories within particular tribes, but the sense of home, of belonging within one's known environment among one's own kin, was absolutely central to all individuals within the tribe. Tribes are aggregates of families and an individual within a tribe is defined by the mores and practices of that tribe. Complicated ties of duty and responsibility as well as rights and privileges within tribes keep its members within the structure. In this respect language is probably of secondary importance. After all, within the remnants of Celtic warrior society that survived in the Scottish Highlands until the mid-eighteenth century there were many clans, or tribes, all of whom spoke Gaelic, who were traditional allies over considerable periods, while others were traditional enemies, despite having a common language. Back in the sixth century when most of western and much of northern Britain was inhabited by people speaking the same, or similar, P-Celtic languages the dialectal variations from tribe to tribe, or area to area, could have been considerable. We also know from several Roman sources that Roman Britain was attacked by groups of Picts and Scots, apparently speaking different Celtic languages, who were joined at a later date by Germanic speakers like the Angles. In respect of the Germanic speakers we should remember that when the Romans brought considerable numbers of troops from the Low Countries into Britain, people had been crossing in both directions over the North Sea for millennia, just as they had been travelling the Megalithic sea routes along the Atlantic coasts. In terms of the relationships between these different peoples I think it of fundamental importance that tribal alliances should not be interpreted in terms of later historical developments like nation states, kingship and feudalism.

It has long been standard practice among historians to treat orally transmitted material as inherently untrustworthy. That this arises from Western society's reliance on literacy need not be doubted. However, it is a position that is hardly tenable. It seems obvious that within oral society the process of education, particularly for the young, and the preservation of a wide variety of lore relating to weather, hunting, agriculture, healing, geography, animal husbandry, inter-human relationships, and all other areas of human activity, would hardly be left to chance. There are early references to the Druids being trained to develop their memories and becoming capable of prodigious feats of recall. Even today amongst storytellers lacking the ability to read or write the amount of material they carry is sometimes staggering. We seem to have developed an attitude that sees our ancestors as being more stupid than ourselves as if the constant technological developments of the past couple of millennia have been matched by an increased level of intelligence and awareness amongst humans. The widespread environmental degradation and pollution of our planet caused by this adherence to technology shows just how unlikely that is. The truth seems to be that within oral societies the need for accurate, dateable material was subjugated to the need for stories and tales that could help preserve the internal cohesion of particular societies. This meant that in some cases the character of a story could change as long as the meaning of the particular tale continued, or was even enhanced by replacing an ancient figure with a new, better known one, for example a more recent ancestor. Making the ancestors the focus of story and/or ritual is a simple method to preserve and emphasise continuity within the family group and their territory – an efficient means of continuing social stabilisation that has been called ancestor worship. It is within both the literate traditions of history and what we know of the traditional oral tales that have come down to us that we can see a picture of Arthur.

When white men first reached Australia they encountered a people who had no literacy as they understood it. The various codes inherent in much aboriginal painting were in fact a symbolic language but the Australian tribes were dependant on oral transmission for much of their cultural continuity. Over the next couple of centuries, stories that Australia had once been inhabited by giant marsupials, like wombats and kangaroos, which the ancestor people had actually hunted, were dismissed by Western-educated academics as dreamtime fantasy – the dreamtime being where much Australian aboriginal myth and legend takes place. That was until the evidence for such creatures began to be discovered at mining sites in the twentieth century. The discoveries of fossil remains of these creatures led to the creation of a new genus of extinct animals called the Diprotodons who last walked the earth over 20,000 years ago. The tribespeople of Australia remembered these creatures for all that time because their tribal units had survived that long and handed down their knowledge over the generations. This clearly shows that orally transmitted material has to be given greater credence than it has been up until now. Storytelling is not like religious formulae where the effect is dependant on the exact repetition of specific words, some of whose meaning can have been lost. Some modern storytellers, however, do prefer to utilise this type of repetition. Within pre-literate societies the role of storytelling is also of much more significance than just 'entertainment'. And if the aboriginal peoples of Australia can transmit accurate information over millennia, why should we not consider the peoples of Dark Age Britain as having that same capacity? Even within supposedly Christianised areas storytelling has continued to flourish, often alongside folklore rituals whose origin derives from pagan times. Many quite common superstitions are in fact originally derived from such pagan roots.

It seems to me that local Arthurian traditions in Scotland should at least be considered as worthy of investigation. Some historians, shackled to the notion of the supremacy of literacy, have suggested that Arthurian stories in various parts of Scotland owe their origin to local landowners renaming their lands because they had read Malory's *Morte d'Arthur* or later romantic versions of the Arthur story. No-one has put forward the same idea regarding other types of storytelling motifs that are in fact universal. Also, as far as I am aware no proof of this suggestion has ever been forthcoming. One of the most notable instances of this is the widespread rejection of Arthur's Seat in Edinburgh as anything other than a literary allusion. As an example of this type of thinking, R. S. Loomis suggested that the twelfth- and thirteenth-century designation of Edinburgh as The Castle of Maidens, a widespread Arthurian referent, was because King David I of Scotland had read Geoffrey of Monmouth's *The History of the Kings of Britain*. The evidence he presented for this was that Robert of Gloucester was a patron of Geoffrey's and undoubtedly had a copy of the book, which Loomis suggests he lent to David, who was so impressed he changed the name of his capital city to The Castle of Maidens. As I have shown elsewhere (in *The Quest for The Nine Maidens*) there is a great deal of evidence for the name The Castle of Maidens originating in the Dark Ages, but this has not stopped many historians from continuing to believe that Scottish Arthurian locations must have arisen from literary sources. This is because received opinion is that Arthur originated in Wales so he could not have originated in Scotland. This despite the fact that in the Dark Age period under consideration there was no such entity as either Scotland or Wales and nation states were still several generations away from coming into existence.

Like all other types of information, the oral tradition must be treated critically and used in conjunction with other disciplines such as written history, archaeology and, I would suggest, place name analysis. It is certainly unfashionable to consider place names as having much to tell us about mythology and legend. This is partly because of the attitudes just described, but I believe that our landscape retains clues as to what our ancestors believed and I shall draw upon a variety of locations to present what I consider to be the background against which we can begin to discern a clearer picture of who the original Arthur was, and what he did.

As we shall see there is a great deal of evidence for endemic battle between the Celtic-speaking tribes in Britain – battle not war. It seems clear that the tribes had the capacity to band together when threatened by outside forces too strong for any individual tribe to combat. This happened in 80 AD when the Romans fought the massed Caledonians at Mons Graupius and nearly two millennia later the Highland tribes gathered together to support Charles Edward Stuart's doomed attempt to regain the British crown, a campaign that put the final nails in the coffin of tribal society in Great Britain. It is from this tribal background that I believe we can see Arthur arising, though, as I hope to show, there are strong grounds for believing he was not resisting invaders but was involved in something that in the long run was every bit as important. In the battles attributed to him he is presented as fighting peoples who were almost all pagan, while he himself has been portrayed as the essence of a Christian knight. While the feudal notion of knighthood is a later addition to the corpus of Arthurian material, the idea of Arthur as being an early crusader for Christ amongst the people of north Britain in the sixth century has much to recommend it.

Before looking at what the various types of sources have to tell us, an attempt should be made to gain some understanding of what sixth-century Britain, and especially its northern parts, was like. The idea of the warrior Celt exemplified by the great Arthur has to be taken with a large handful of salt. What we can say about the population of the British Isles even back in the sixth century is that it was probably quite mixed. We know of the arrivals of people from Scandinavia and the Low Countries over considerable periods of historical time but what matters more is that the archaeological record shows that the peoples around the North Sea, and up and down the Atlantic coasts, were in contact with each other thousands of years before the Romans came. None of this is to downplay the importance of the Celtic-speaking society in which Arthur probably grew up. As we shall see, this society was in some ways distinctive while in other ways not much different from other tribal societies in contemporary Continental Europe.

The world that Arthur inhabited in sixth-century Britain was a world undergoing change. Britain had seen invasion by the Roman armies and the arrival of a new religion, Christianity, in the period up to the sixth century, but the idea that the people of these islands were part of some sort of primitive society unaware of the rest of the world before contact with Mediterranean peoples is unsustainable. Life in the north of Britain at the dawn of the sixth century was much different from even a few centuries later. There were no cities, people lived in small, kin-based groups on the most fertile ground and much of the island was impassable because of bog and thick forest.

Chapter Two

The Sixth-Century Background

BY THE EARLY YEARS of the sixth century much of England had already seen extensive urban development and the growth of centralised power under the Romans. Even after the Romans left some towns continued to function as local centres of power. In parts of England, most of Wales and virtually all of Scotland this had not happened and the people still lived as they had done for generations. The peoples we know were here have come down to us essentially defined by the languages they spoke, a situation that causes some problems in trying to disentangle what we can find out about the period.

In *The Gododdin of Aneurin* (p. xx), J. T. Koch makes the point:

> We must bear in mind that there was at the time [close to the end of the sixth century] no political entity which was even approximately co-extensive with the ethno-linguistic collectivity of the Britons nor with that of the Anglo-Saxons. In both societies the primary institutions of political power were chieftain, dynasty, court and tribe. In the short-term interests of the lord (this being often the same as his survival), a rigid ethno-linguistic barrier for potential military followers and alliances could invite disaster.

This makes a great deal of sense and he goes on to describe the make-up of contemporary Britain in terms which are much more relevant to a tribal society rather than anything like a modern nation state. He tells us:

> For the sixth and seventh centuries, at least, it is a matter of disunited, small scale dynastic polities on both sides [I would substitute tribal for dynastic]. It is fundamentally wrong , and in fact ludicrous, to conceive of the English settlements and expansion as a great war of some 300

years in duration in which a monolithic Brittonic nation purposefully resisted the advance of a comparable monolithic Germanic invader. The greater issue before historians of the Migration Period is not, therefore, the strategies of a conquest and the resistance to it, but the slower and less colourful working out of an ethno-linguistic shift during a pro-longed period of endemic and ambivalent political violence. (p. xliii)

In the Dark Ages, the name given to the period between the Romans quitting Britain in 410 AD and roughly the year 1000 AD, there are indeed few literary sources that tell us what life was like. We do have some Roman records but those relating to Scotland are rather few in number. While England was part of the Roman Empire for several hundred years, Scotland was only partially occupied, and for relatively short periods of time. We know there were several Roman expeditions to the far north but even the area between the Antonine Wall and Hadrian's Wall was little more than an extended frontier of the Roman Empire. Because of the development of British history, an inordinate amount of attention has been paid to the Romans in Scotland. No one can deny they must have had a considerable influence particularly in the area between the walls, but many of the military structures still to be seen in Scotland's landscape were little more than marching camps. Recent research has raised the possibility that the primary role of the Antonine Wall and other Roman occupation sites in Scotland was to protect trade routes. The ongoing influence of Roman rule in Scotland has been assumed by many commentators but I would suggest that the biggest impact they had in the north of Britain was in fact the introduction of Christianity, which can be seen as particularly influential in the development of the proto-kingdoms of north Britain from the sixth century onwards.

Much of the interpretation of the nearest contemporary records has concentrated on the role of kingship and I think that this is misplaced. The societies of this period were essentially tribal and functioned through kin-groups of which the chiefs were a part. Their role depended on their relationship with the rest of the tribe, their own kin, and we should try to understand contemporary society on the basis of kinship, not kingship. The specific role of Christianity in the political and social life of the period can be seen in the behaviour of various sixth-century clerics. St Columba was expelled from his native Ireland for causing a battle by illicitly making a copy of a religious document. He came to Scotland and set up his community on Iona, even then an island of ancient sanctity. Before long he was directly involved in the politics of Dalriada, the area of Argyll on Scotland's west coast that was inhabited by Gaelic-speaking Scots. Claiming he had been sent a dream by God, he succeeded in putting his own favoured candidate in control. Most commentators have followed Adomnan in saying that he made Aedan Mac Gabhran king, instead of his brother Eoganan. Adomnan, trained within the Christian church, had all the conditioning of the classical outlook. I think the use of the term king here is misleading; Aedan is more likely to have had a role as a tribal chief, with possibly an overall position over a group of tribes. These tribes have survived in the classification of the different groups of Dalriada as Cenell Comgaill, Cenell Loarn, Cenell nGabhrain, and Cenell nOengusa, the term Cenell meaning family. Each of these four groupings claimed descent from a particular individual which is classic tribal practice. While we have no records of how kinship structures were organised amongst the Britons and Picts in sixth-century Scotland, it is likely that they were organised along similar lines to the Scots of Dalriada. Evidence from Ireland casts some light on how such societies would have been structured. For most legal and day-to-day purposes the kin-group was defined as four generations of the same family, claiming descent from a common great-grandparent. Land was owned jointly by the group and all had shares in inheritance and also in obligations. A similar type of system appears to have operated among the Welsh tribes. Within tribal structures there was no guarantee of succession to chieftainship of the chief's eldest son, as has been noted. In fact uncles and various nephews would have as much right to the succession, which meant that there was a choice as to who would be the best candidate. This also applied to the favourite occupation of the men of these tribes – battle. The leader in battle would be the most skilled and able man available, otherwise the efficiency of the group would be impaired, with potentially disastrous results for the entire tribe. We must remember that all of these people were related and lived in what were effectively extended families. Within such groups everyone knows everyone else's faults, and abilities. What we know from late British tribal society, within the Highland clan system, makes it clear that a chief would have to show his skills in battle or raiding, but that he would not be expected to lead in every battle, unless he was the best candidate available. This is probably why Arthur became such a hero – he was chosen as the fittest to lead a war band that was particularly large, and especially victorious.

Tribal Areas in Post-Roman Scotland

In the centuries after the Romans left Britain, what we now call Scotland was occupied by several different groups of people. Historians have tended to call these groups kingdoms or nations. In one sense perhaps they were nations – just as the tribal peoples of North America referred to themselves as nations. These nations were the Britons of Strathclyde, an area stretching from just north of the Clyde down the west coast probably as far as Carlisle. Dumbarton Rock and other sites such as Dundonald in Ayrshire were of particular significance, though whether we can see them as capitals in the modern sense is a moot point. Also on the west coast and somewhere near modern south Ayrshire was a smaller nation, Rheged, though much discussion still rages over precisely where this was. In eastern southern Scotland, running from the Forth as far south as the Tees, at their most extensive were the Gododdin, the tribal people referred to by the second-century Greek geographer Ptolemy as the Votadini. There are references in early Welsh sources to Manau Gododdin, an area which seems to have included the lands on the south side of the Forth east of Edinburgh. Again it is difficult to define the specific area but there are reasons for seeing Manau Gododdin as including some of the lands on the north side of the Forth around Clackmannan and possibly on the south side of the river stretching up towards the headwaters of the Forth. Within this area Edinburgh Castle Rock, Stirling Castle Rock and Traprain Law near Haddington were all of strategic and cultural importance.

North of the Forth were the Picts, who seem to have been divided into northern and southern confederations. The Picts have long been considered a historical enigma but recent research shows them to have been much like their neighbours. What sets them apart is the magnificent corpus of carved Symbol Stones from both pagan and Christian times. Like the Britons of Strathclyde and Manau they were a P-Celtic-speaking people and even the suggestion that they might have practised matriliny – descent through the female line – need not necessarily differentiate them much from the other peoples of the time. In this regard it is significant that we have Arthurian tales and place names from Pictish areas. On the west in modern Argyll, centred on the hilltop site of Dunadd in the middle of Kilmartin valley, were the Scots of Dalriada. They were a Q-Celtic-speaking people probably in regular contact with other Q-Celtic-speaking tribes in Ireland. It seems more than likely that the Scots controlled many of the islands of the Inner Hebrides. Given the length of experience of sea travel in the area, they were likely to have been capable sailors and would have used the seas and rivers for communication and trade. Regular road communication in Scotland was hundreds of years in the future. All of these peoples seem to have been essentially similar – they lived in self-sufficient, small, family groups, raised cattle, grew some crops, and were fond of hunting. The role of the warrior, which would include all fit adult males, was probably much the same in all of these societies, and their social relationships within and between the different tribes were defined by their family or kinship relationships.

Roman sources tell of raiding across the walls by combined forces of Picts and Scots. This shows their capacity to work together and in the ensuing centuries there were several instances when Dalriadan Scots actually became 'kings' of the Picts. This might have been due to a process whereby a 'king' was created by marrying the queen, who represented the dynastic line. This is echoed in Ireland where kings were said to have married a representative of sovereignty. In *Celtic Heritage* (p. 74) A. and B. Rees tell us the following:

> The relation between Irish kings and their realms is often portrayed as a marriage and the inauguration feast of a king called a wedding-feast. The country is a woman, the spouse of the king, and before her marriage she is a hag, or a woman whose mind is deranged. When she is united with the king her countenance is 'as the crimson lichen of Leinster's crags . . . her locks like Bregon's buttercups, her mantle a matchless green'.

In fact, this is much more like marriage to a goddess or the representative of a goddess embodying the concept of the country or land itself, and the reference to the hag changing to the beautiful bride is something that links closely to central motifs in the pagan religion. We shall meet the hag again.

The P-Celtic-speaking peoples of Strathearn and the Lennox in west central Scotland lived close to the lands of Q-Celtic speakers in Dalriada and they obviously could, and did, co-operate when it was seen to be to their mutual advantage. The modern stress on defining peoples by what language they speak has blinded too many historians to this. It also puts a rather different perspective on the eventual amalgamation of the Picts and Scots under Kenneth MacAlpin in the ninth century. The nineteenth-century historian W. F. Skene, who was extremely interested in matters Arthurian, went so far as to suggest that the stories of Arthur amongst the Britons and the story of Finn MacCoul among the Gaels might have originated in the area where these two different groups lived alongside each other, and thus might have had a common root.

All of these peoples were economically self-sufficient tribal societies living in small family groups and several Roman commentators noted the lack of urban development. The idea that they were geographically and culturally isolated hardly bears scrutiny. Trade in gold and amber had meant communications with Scandinavia, the Low Countries and the lands of south-western Europe for a very long time, and before that there had been the communication routes of the Megalithic builders. Professor Barry Cunliffe in *Facing the Ocean* clearly shows there was flourishing trade and communication along the eastern coasts of the Atlantic Ocean from Megalithic times onwards. With the ease of travel by sea at certain times of the year, and the fact that before extensive forest clearance and drainage much of the land would have proved very difficult to travel through, it seems obvious that the seas and rivers would have been the natural means of travel and communication. This also means that contact with Wales and Ireland would have been nothing out of the ordinary. As far back as 3500 BC people were sailing along the Atlantic coasts. Cunliffe (p. 183) makes a telling point: 'eastern and much of southern Britain shared in a broad North Sea cultural continuum. The henge monuments, on the other hand, appear to be a more insular phenomenon, and, given their early appearance in Orkney, it is possible that the religious motivation behind these constructions may first have originated in the northern part of the Atlantic zone.' This is significant in the continuum of religious belief that existed before the Romans invaded Britain and the subsequent arrival of Christianity. While England had been under centralised rule with towns, good communications and growing literacy under Roman rule, the Romans were never in Scotland long enough for any of these to develop. The growth of Christianity in England was associated with already developed urban centres. There had been a considerable move away from traditional tribal structures in the four centuries of Roman rule. Things were different north of Hadrian's Wall.

The key to understanding what sixth-century society in Scotland was like lies in appreciating that the social structure was tribal. As early as the first century AD, Tacitus in *Agricola* makes it clear that the leader of the Caledonians was not a king. His name, Calgacus, translates as The Swordsman, and this would be a fitting title, or even name, for someone who was a war-leader. What we know of the Scottish Highland clans and other tribal societies suggests that such leaders were appointed for their martial skills rather than anything to do with their genealogy, which would of course not stop anyone in the position of chief from leading his people, or even a confederation of tribes, if he was the best available war-leader. The problem with Tacitus, as with many other early sources, is that we lack corroboration of what he says, and he himself was transmitting information second-hand. He never was in Britain and was writing in praise of his father-in-law Agricola, the leader of the Roman army in Britain. When writing such basic works in praise of an individual it is of course a good idea to present the enemies of the subject as both capable and courageous. Tacitus (*On Britain and Germany*, pp. 79f.) tells us Calgacus spoke these words:

> Whenever I consider why we are fighting and how we have reached this crisis, I have a strong sense that this day of your splendid rally may mean the dawn of liberty for the whole of Britain. You have mustered to a man and to a man you are free ... We, the last men on earth, the last of the free, have been shielded till today by the very remoteness and seclusion for which we are famed ... Brigands of the world they have exhausted the land by their indiscriminate plunder, and now they ransack the sea ... Robbery, butchery, rapine, the liars call Empire; they create a desolation and call it peace.

This seems a bit too much like Roman oratory to be taken as a verbatim report of what was said, but in the sense that tribal peoples defined themselves by the territory they occupied, it reflects the reality that they would, at the least, put up a good fight. This would make them worthwhile opponents for the noble Agricola as Tacitus presents him. Here we have a panegyric – a work written in praise of a particular individual – accepted as a historical record because there is nothing else of the same period about north Britain in existence. The main point here is that Calgacus was not a king, and there seems to be no doubt that he was leading a coalition of different tribes, united in opposition to an invading army. What Tacitus tells us is in essence no more reliable than the material arising from the early Welsh poems supposedly composed by Taliesin and Aneurin; such poems deriving from oral traditions can have a great deal to teach us. N. Chadwick in *The British Heroic Age* (pp. 70f.) makes a significant point about the role of early poems:

> As there were no newspapers these panegyric poems had enormous propaganda value . . . The elegiac poems served the interest of the heirs, by their praise of the great deeds of the ancestors . . . Like the poems of Homer they are interested solely in individuals; they have no conception of a state, or of politics, or of a policy. Their warfare and their enemies are also personal.

Here the personal can be seen as relating directly to family: they may have no sense of state or politics in the modern sense but they would have a highly developed awareness of inter-relationships within their own kin-group, and probably also between their own kin-group and others. Consistently the activities of the few individuals mentioned in sources from, or concerned with, the Dark Ages in Scotland have been interpreted as if they were kings. The first dateable reference to Arthur makes no mention of any rank whatsoever. *The Gododdin* says: 'Gwawrddur would feed black ravens on the wall of a fortress, though he were not Arthur.' Here, feeding the ravens means being successful in battle as the ravens come to the battlefield, here a fortress, to pick at the bodies of the slain.

The Gododdin survived amongst the Welsh-speaking tribes of north Wales and might have been written down as early as the seventh century. It is quite likely that the poem survived in Strathclyde and Wales for a few centuries after its composition in around about 600 AD, perhaps in both written and oral forms. Much of Welsh tradition from the Dark Age period concerns the Gwr Y Gogledd, the Men of the North, the ancestors of the tribes who moved down to Wales at different times between the fifth and eighth centuries from central Scotland. The warriors of *The Gododdin* are accepted as being part of the Men of the North. In sixth-century north Britain we have several distinct societies which have generally been interpreted as kingdoms, an analysis which is anachronistic, though some of them did eventually develop into kingdoms. The most important of these was probably Strathclyde, whose people, like the Gododdin and the Picts to the north, spoke a P-Celtic language, recently referred to as Common Archaic Neo-Brittonic, quite a mouthful but a fair description of a language continuum stretching from Scotland to France. J. T. Koch applies the term to the geographical area from the rivers Forth to the Loire but I would suggest that this should be extended north to include those areas of Scotland occupied by the Picts. This would include the Orkney and Shetland Islands. There is no doubt that Strathclyde came under strong Christian influence, perhaps from as early as the fifth century AD, though its most famous saint, Kentigern, is linked in many ways to earlier pagan traditions. He is said to have been a direct contemporary of Columba who came to Scotland in 635. It is in *Life of Kentigern* that we have what is probably the earliest reference to another figure who becomes central to later medieval and post-medieval Arthurian romance. The story is told of a bardic figure who goes mad after the Battle of Caledon. In the *Life of Kentigern* he is referred to as Lailoken and many scholars see him as the original of the magical figure of Merlin. Much has been made of the supposed leader, or patron, of the war band in the *The Gododdin*, one Mynydawc Mwynvawr. As we shall see this powerful prince, or chief, possibly did not exist at all.

Chieftainship and Tribalism

The concept of the chief is of vital importance in understanding the period in which the historical Arthur was active. Chiefs are not kings; kings rule over their societies, chiefs rule on behalf of their societies, who are after all composed mainly of their relatives. We know from many sources that there was a strong element of election within the leadership of the Celtic-speaking tribes of Britain and that some of their practices, such as succession by brothers, might be a remnant of a matrilineal system. Though the elective aspect of kingship in no way suggests a democratic structure within Scottish Dark Age tribal societies it does prove that there was nothing remotely feudal about the way people lived. The overall concept seems to be that the chief would be chosen as the best available candidate from among those with the entitlement to lead the tribe, or clan. Such a decision would not always have been universally popular and disputes undoubtedly arose.

The idea of the chief as the leader of the tribe and ultimately responsible to the tribe is borne out by evidence from the eighteenth century in the dying years of the Highland clan system. This is from Edward Burt's *Letters From A Gentleman in the North of Scotland* (1 p. 109), written in the 1730s. He is describing what happened when he met a Highland chief who had boasted of his power over his clansmen on a visit to England and was then in turn visited by one of his English acquaintances:

And as the meanest among them pretend to be his Relations by Consanguinity, they insist upon the Privilege of taking him by the Hand whenever they meet him. Concerning this last, I once saw a Number of very discontented Countenances when a certain Lord, one of the Chiefs, endeavoured to evade this Ceremony. It was in Presence of an English Gentleman in high station, from whom he would have willingly have concealed the Knowledge of such seeming Familiarity with slaves of so wretched Appearance, and thinking it, I suppose, as a kind of Contradiction to what he had often boasted at other Times, viz., his despotic Power over his Clan.

Coming from a period more than sixteen hundred years after the Romans are said to have met the massed ranks of the Caledonians at Mons Graupius circa 80 AD, this is remarkable proof of the longevity of tribal existence within Scotland. Effectively, in the eighteenth century, the Highland clan system remained at its core an Iron Age warrior society, with an essentially subsistence economy, living alongside a modern, mercantile and rapidly industrialising nation state.

Another remarkable attestation to the tribalism of sixth-century north British society comes from the Pictish Symbol Stones. These remarkable monuments are generally dated as being created from the seventh century onwards, though as yet this is theoretical, and based upon comparisons with art styles elsewhere. Given that we know the peoples of north Britain had a long history of contacts with far-flung areas, the idea that the Picts were isolated until the Romans arrived and that they were heirs only to outside influence in the fifth to seventh centuries is hard to sustain. Cultural contacts are never completely one way, despite the Empire mentality of nineteenth-century Europeans, and the dating of the Pictish stones might yet be pushed backwards. However, even if they do come from the seventh century onwards they are undoubtedly the closest contemporary visual records of warriors, and in one case of battle, that we have in looking at the Arthurian period. Dr Paul Wagner of the Stoccata School of Defence in New South Wales, Australia, recently pointed out to me that the portrayals of Pictish

Matriliny

There is ongoing debate as to whether the Picts practised matriliny, the system whereby a king or chief by would inherit his status from his mother rather than his father. Such a system would see brother succeeding brother and succession would devolve to a sister's son thereafter. Parts of this system lasted well into the eleventh century when Malcolm Canmore's sons succeeded each other (even as late as this time there was no guaranteed primogeniture), the succession by the eldest son. There has been an implicit assumption on the part of many historians that succession by the eldest son was the norm in tribal societies. In this respect the Pictish king-list provides a useful comparison. In not one instance is a father succeeded by a son though there are several occasions where a brother follows brother. It has recently been suggested by Kyle Gray in *The Pictish Arts Society Journal* (no. 10, pp. 7f.) that some of the parental names given in the king-list are in fact female. Some of the kings in the list were not Pictish but were brought in from among the Scots or Britons of Strathclyde. If such a system existed amongst the Pictish peoples, is it not possible that it was also the norm in some of the other P-Celtic-speaking tribes of central and southern Scotland at this time? In Ireland the kings were said to have married a female representation of sovereignty which, though interpreted as marriage to a representative of the Goddess, Eriu, herself representing Ireland, might refer to something similar existing amongst the Gaels.

warriors show them to be armed with weapons for fighting one on one. They have either short swords or spears and small shields or bucklers. The shields are either round or square, but are all small. The contrast with the heavy shields of Roman troops is startling. What this means is that the type of fighting they were involved in was essentially hand to hand, one warrior against another. This conforms to what we know of battle practice in late Scottish Highland society. Effectively what these carved stones show us is that the Pictish warriors, P-Celtic-speaking near contemporaries of Arthur and the Britons, were involved primarily in battle, not war.

Martin Martin, who visited the western islands of Scotland in the late seventeenth century, stated in *A Description of the Western Isles of Scotland* (p. 248) that amongst the clansmen 'the ancient way of fighting was by set battles'. Such types of fighting are more about individual and tribal honour than conquest or domination, and if not exactly ritual warfare are certainly very formalised.

Again late Highland society showed this in the Cateran or cattle-raiding tradition. Here the young men of the tribe (the famous Fianna of Irish and Scottish Gaelic lore are perhaps modelled directly on tribal practice) would be trained as warriors and at a particular time of the year, the autumn, would set out to raid the cattle of other clans. Cattle were the main form of obvious dis-posable wealth and had been since the Iron Age. Obviously they would travel some distance because if they raided their neighbours there would be little possibility of substantial gain – the neighbours would notice and respond, leading in all likelihood to open and continuing warfare. The idea seems to have been that they should prove their skills by lifting cattle and transporting them back, sometimes over hundreds of miles. If they were discovered or were followed and caught up with, battle would certainly ensue. It also seems as if all of the able males of the clan were warriors. John Major in *A History of Greater Britain*, published in 1521, tells of Highland tenants who 'keep a horse and weapons of war, and are ready to take part in his quarrel, be it just or unjust, if they only have a liking for him, if need be, to fight to the death.' Here he is referring to the chief and this shows how different tribal society was, not just from feudal society but from the rapidly developing modern society of Britain as a whole. Under feudalism they would have had no right to refuse to fight on behalf of their superior, yet here there is the telling qualification 'if only they have a liking for him'.

The type of battle amongst the Highland clans again shows how different tribal society was from feudal and later structures.

The Battle of Saughs which took place around 1700 in the Glens of Angus, north of the River Tay, proves a case in point. This story is taken originally from A. Jervise's *The Land of the Lindsays* (pp. 258f.). Although by this period clan tribal society was in sharp decline, a bunch of Caterans, or Highland raiders had come down from Deeside to raid the village of Fearn in Strathmore. They managed to round up most of the local stock and head up Glen Lethnot towards home before the inhabitants of Fearn and the area awoke. When they did awake a party was quickly formed and, arming themselves, went in pursuit. The raiders were caught up with near the head of the Burn of Saughs. The leaders of the Fearn men were James Macintosh of Ledenhendrie and James Wilson, both known for their admiration of the traditional warrior ways of the clans – something which almost cost them dear. On catching up with the raiders Ledenhendrie was challenged to single combat by the leader of the Deeside men, a veritable giant, all of two metres tall who went by the name of the Hawkit Stirk (a name previously used by a very famous Cateran and meaning the white-faced steer). According to the ancient ways Ledenhendrie had no choice but to accept and if he lost the cattle would be taken north, despite the fact the Fearn men were more numerous and better armed than their foes. In the ensuing sword fight Ledenhendrie could not overcome the advantage his opponent's vast reach gave him and was asked to yield. This he refused to do and it seemed he would be killed. Luckily, for him at least, a hare started out of the heather and ran between the two groups of men. One of the Highlanders shouted in Gaelic, 'It's a witch' and fired his musket at it (witches were reputed to often change into hares) but his aim was bad. He missed the hare and killed one of the Fearn men, so wholesale battle commenced. This allowed Winter to dispatch the Hawkit Stirk from behind and the Deesidemen were all killed. This I believe illustrates very clearly the tenacity of the ancient tribal warrior beliefs – Ledenhendrie was prepared to die rather then have his honour besmirched. This finds an echo in Geoffrey of Monmouth's *The History of the Kings of Britain* where in the section on Arthur of Britain (p. 224) he tells of Arthur's struggle with an enemy king, Frollo:

> Frollo grieved to see his people dying of hunger, and sent a message to Arthur to say that they should meet in single combat and that whichever was victorious should take the kingdom of the other.

This sense of honour is found in other tribal societies. An example can be seen in the Plains tribes of North America and the habit of counting coup. This was when a warrior showed his bravery by riding into battle with the head of his lance removed and the shaft tied into a curve at the end with the intention of striking one or more of the enemy with the harmless weapon before riding back. This showed his skill and his bravery, and had the advantage of demeaning the opposing warriors who had been struck. This insistence on skill and bravery was the same in the British tribes which meant that only a leader worthy of his place would be followed by the men of the tribe. The men of the tribe were all trained as warriors, but unless they went off to fight abroad as mercenaries, were never soldiers. The clans, like tribes everywhere, fought when there was something they thought worth fighting for – even if from the point of view of adjoining non-tribal societies their raiding for booty would be seen as nothing more or less than thieving. This also raises the possibility that the later Arthurian romances were in fact heavily influenced by tribal mores and might not be as significantly influenced by idealised concepts of feudalism as generally supposed.

W. F. Skene in *The Highlanders of Scotland* makes the point that the people in a tribe, or clan, followed their chief, who as the leader of their group represented the common ancestor of all of them. This could hardly be further from the feudal concept of following a leader to whom they were obligated as the owner of the lands on which they lived, and which they had been given in return for specific military duty. The hierarchic structure of feudalism stretched all the way up to the king who was supreme over the entire population and answerable only to God. Chieftainship was on behalf of the community, not over it. M. Gluckman in *Politics, Law and Ritual in Tribal Society* (p. 40) tells us: 'The right of all subjects to claim sufficient land, as an inherent attribute of citizenship, marked the political systems of the Ancient Germans and Celts, and not the land-tenure system of feudalism.' The raiders or Caterans in our tale were carrying out a traditional procedure in lifting the cattle of other clans. This is thought to have been a constant attribute of the clan system for centuries, possibly since the start of the Iron Age. Gluckman, referring to tribal practice in many parts of the world and over considerable periods of time, goes on to tell us: 'Herds of cattle are nuclei round which kinship groups are clustered and the relationships between their members operate through cattle and are expressed in terms of cattle.' (p. 46) This probably accounts for the importance of cattle in early Irish sagas and I would suggest that in sixth-century Britain things would have been much the same. We also know that the reliance of the Highlanders on their 'black cattle' lasted until the eighteenth century. The people of the sixth-century tribes in Scotland seem to have lived in much the same way as their descendants.

Most of the earliest commentators on the Arthurian period and the Dark Ages in general use the term king as if referring to a feudal type of king. It is obvious that within the tribal societies of the time the over-chief would have had a position as dependant on the lesser chiefs as they were themselves dependent on, and essentially answerable to, their own clan or tribe. Tribalism survived in the clan system until the eighteenth century in the Scottish Highlands, and I think it quite likely that the well-known tradition of reiving, or raiding, in the Scottish Borders was another example of the same type of behaviour shown by the Caterans. The ancestors of the Border raiders were, of course, the people we know of as the Gododdin. Some historians see the rise of the reiving tradition of the border area between Scotland and England as a result of the ongoing battles fought between the two countries from the medieval period onwards. However, when one compares how the Reivers behaved with the actions of the Highland warriors, there do seem to be strong resemblances. In the Borders the raiding parties were from families – Kerrs, Nixons, Armstrongs and others, kin-groups just like the clans – and these kin-groups continued to resist the power of centralising authority as long as they could. Their loyalties were to their own – a consistent and fundamental aspect of all tribal society. A quote from James Rennie's *The Scottish People* (p. 229) illustrates the point: 'Both used oatmeal, two-handed broadswords and targe, both have slogans and both loved the hunt, especially for deer.' Rennie makes the point that in times of peace reiving had specific rules, again similar to the practices of the Highland warriors, and 'to be completely successful, a raid had to be carried out without the fatal shedding of blood.' (Ibid.) This suggests that fighting could have taken place and, as in the case of the Battle of Saughs, could have been one on one, or single combat, and not necessarily to the death. One of the problems we have in trying to understand this material is that almost all of the early records we have concerning raiding from Border and Highland areas come from those being raided, and these victims were certainly non-tribal. The great fear of Highlanders and Border Reivers among the general population of Lowland Scotland can be seen in the light of a total incapacity on either side to comprehend just how the others lived. This in part explains why the late cattle-raiding by Highlanders from the fifteenth century onwards survives in most records as plain theft. In the eyes of the Highland raiders this was certainly not the case. H. Howlett in *Highland Constable* (p. 17) explains the attitude towards such raiding in the seventeenth century: 'Like poaching in England, it had public opinion very largely behind it, and was commonly justified on the grounds that there can be no ownership of living beasts. If it was dishonest then the dishonesty was on a noble scale, the next thing to real war.' This presentation of the cattle-raiding traditions of the Highland clans as theft was particularly strong in the aftermath of Culloden in 1746 when the Highland army was defeated by the British army. Several hundred of the Highland army in fact continued to hold out, supporting themselves by their traditional practice of cattle-raiding, though now all the raiding was on Lowland farms. The British army under the command of the Duke of Cumberland was hell bent on destroying the last vestiges of Highland clan society – a society that had grimly held on to its independence despite constant attempts to bring it into line. The Highlanders who fought on seemed to have seen all of the non-Gaelic-speaking population as supporting their enemy, the Hanoverian dynasty, and thus felt justified in carrying out raids on them. The presentation of what was essentially a policy of attempted genocide as a battle against widespread depredations by ruthless thieves was a convenient cover-up.

Another intriguing similarity between the Borders and Highlands suggests this essentially tribal approach. Although we have Tacitus's account of the Battle of Mons Graupius, which some commentators suggest might be pure invention, there are no records of any other set battles between the Romans and the Caledonians or later the Picts. This is despite the fact that there were several Roman expeditions that went as far as the Moray Firth if not further. It is feasible that the tribal warrior bands would see little sense in attacking a passing army unless they could carry out a lightning raid for booty and then escape. The nature of tribal society, and the function of warriors within it, suggests that guerrilla warfare would be their preferred option when dealing with large armies of soldiers trained to fight pitched battles. This could apply equally to the Border clans in the centuries in which battle between Scotland and England was endemic. It is known that some of the Border families fought on both sides at different times, an understandable policy if their loyalty was to the kin group and not to a feudal lord or even to the concept of the nation state. Again this type of behaviour finds echoes as late as 1745–6 when the Highland troops are said to have returned from Derby to get their crops in. Their deepest loyalty was to their own family and clan, not to the Stuart dynasty.

To this day there is argument over where Mons Graupius took place, most commentators accepting that there was an actual battle. Tacitus makes it clear that the battle was against the Caledonians and it is generally accepted that it took place beyond the Antonine Wall. This wall was not raised until around 180 AD; Mons Graupius was fought around 80 AD. There is another fact that has not been much noted. In Arthurian terms no-one who has investigated the early material has ever doubted that the battle referred to as Cat Coit Celidon translates as the Battle in the Caledonian Wood. Further, it is accepted that this wood covered much of the Southern Uplands of Scotland. This is considerably further south than the Antonine Wall. The Caledonians certainly included the people who came to be known as the Picts who are generally considered to have inhabited the lands north of the Forth. Scholarly opinion has little doubt that the Picts were P-Celtic-speaking just as the peoples of Manau Gododdin and Strathclyde were. The Caledonians are referred to by one Roman source as 'Caledonians and other Picts'. In the ninth century the kingdom of Scotland came into being through a merging of the Scots and the Picts into something approaching a nation state under Kenneth MacAlpin. This alliance echoes something that had occurred on a temporary basis many times in the past. Roman sources speak of raids from the north by Picts and Scots and Picts, Scots and Angles. All of these raids can be seen as conforming to temporary tribal alliances just as was the case at Mons Graupius. If the Caledonian Wood derives its name from the same origin as the term Caledonians referring to the people of Scotland then we have the intriguing possibility that Mons Graupius might have been fought in the southern part of Scotland.

Let us return to *The Gododdin*, the poem containing our earliest dateable reference to Arthur, as an exemplary warrior. In *The Gododdin of Aneurin* J. T. Koch suggests that the supposed organiser, or patron, of the battle raid, Mynydawc Mwynvawr, did not exist. He suggests (p. xlvi) that the term means something like 'the luxurious mountain chief' or even 'the luxurious mountain court or hall'. This latter description he thinks could refer directly to Edinburgh's Castle Rock, to which we will return later. He suggests that one of the named warriors in the poem, Urei of Strathclyde, would make a good candidate for a 'luxurious mountain chief' and the leader of the war band. There is, however, another striking fact about the poem. It consists mostly of a list of the fallen. It has been suggested that the original number of warriors who set out on the raid was 300. This is not stated definitely and relies on comparisons with the later Welsh Gorsedd, a troop of 300 horsemen, and the fact that the Romans had troops of 300 cavalry. These are the Romans who had not been in Scotland since 210 AD in any considerable force. The point about this is that the poem mentions 60 different warriors, and we cannot be sure we have the entire poem. The naming of these individuals, few of whom are accorded any rank, suggests they are all important – exactly what one would expect in a tribal situation. Even if there were 300 warriors and we have all of the original poem, why mention 60 of them if this was an expedition organised by some kind of local king, or chief? It makes more sense to see this as an essentially tribal affair in which all of the warriors are important. The interpretation of the Dark Ages as having 'king' figures with an attendant hierarchy of aristocrats, similar in some way to the supremely powerful feudal monarchs of a much later period, blinds us to the realities of what seems to have been going on. To mention all of these warriors means that they were all important to the intended audience. If the poems were created purely for an aristocratic audience why mention so many different warriors? Surely if this was some sort of praise poem to an aristocrat in the post-feudal sense of the word we should have the original bard singing the praises of a particular ancestor or even group of ancestors, or perhaps the direct ancestors of his aristocratic audience. The truth would appear to be that society in north Britain at this time was essentially tribal and had been for a long, long time. In this respect it is worth recalling Burt's description of the clansman and his chief. The lists of ancestors that were regularly recited by the seannachies, the bardic genealogists of the Scottish clans, were not just for the chief's benefit. They referred to the ancestors of all of the people of the clan, the chief's extended family.

Other aspects of what clearly seem to have been tribal practices have been given anachronistic interpretations. Nennius, writing many years after the time of Arthur's death in 539, in the section of his work referred to as the Northern History, says: 'Then Oswy delivered all the riches he had in the city into the hand of Penda, and Penda distributed them to the kings of the British, that is the 'Distribution of Iudeu'.' (p. 38) Iudeu has been interpreted as being somewhere in southern or central Scotland and it is possible it was what is now Stirling. Another possible location for it might be Camelon, near Falkirk. Nennius specifically mentions the various leaders as kings and this event at Iudeu has been interpreted as some sort of giving of gifts to secure allegiance. This is not the only way of looking at it. The giving of gifts is an extremely common form of tribal and inter-tribal behaviour in many parts of the world. Within tribal societies the best-known example of such gift-giving is probably potlatching, a custom among the indigenous tribes of north-western America where ritual activities of gift-giving would result in an individual giving away all of his or her possessions. As other individuals would do the same thing, possession would in fact circulate around the tribe. The amassing of individual wealth within a tribe is a dangerous activity and the wealth of a tribe or kin-group was held in common, even if to outsiders it might all appear to belong to the chief. The same sort of gift-giving happened between tribes. It was a means of reinforcing long-established patterns of duties and obligations within the relevant group and bears no relation to the pledging of feudal allegiance. Another cautionary point is that Nennius was a Christian-trained scribe – his education arose from classical sources, not from any indigenous tradition or knowledge. This is extremely significant because the growth of the nation state in succeeding centuries was heavily influenced by Christianity.

Invasions

Until comparatively recently the portrayal of fifth- to seventh-century British history was dominated by the theory of invasions. The Anglo-Saxons were supposed to have invaded *en masse* after Hengist and Horsa were invited in by Vortigern in the fifth century to help defend the Britons against the Picts and Scots. On the west of Scotland, the Scots of Dalriada were said to have invaded from Ireland *circa* 500 AD. Modern archaeology has shown both these ideas to be untenable. The migration of Germanic-speakers from the Low Countries and elsewhere in Europe had been going on steadily since the Romans brought over Germanic-speaking troops as early as the first century AD. The so-called Anglo-Saxon invasion really rests on one source, Gildas, who is otherwise considered rather untrustworthy. The references to barbarian conspiracies and other alliances attacking the Roman walls all suggest an ongoing, if irregular relationship between Celtic- and Germanic-speaking tribes. We have no idea whether there was close contact between them even earlier than the Roman period but it is a possibility that is hard to rule out. It has also been realised that the Scots of

Dalriada were settled in Argyll and much of the Western Isles of Scotland long before the sixth century. They could even have been as native to north Britain as the Picts and, despite ongoing attempts to show that people with the sophisticated stone and metal-working skills of the Picts and Scots must have originated outside Scotland, the evidence suggests they were essentially indigenous. After all, such Megalithic structures as Calanais, The Rings of Brodgar and Stenness and the magnificent Maes Howe were all raised over three millennia before Arthur was born. While there is no doubt the Romans did invade and conquer southern Britian most other so-called invasions have little to support them. Even such an important landmark event in English history as the Norman invasion was really a dynastic struggle and did not involve large-scale population movements. For a long time British archaeologists tended to analyse technical developments as a result of outside influence and to this day the arrival of the Celtic languages is still suggested to have come about because of an invasion. The idea of such invasions is usually that a technologically superior group of peoples arrives and subjugates the local populace. It has been quite normal to assume that such invaders if not already living in a hierarchically structured society became overlords of the original population. This is the same approach that interprets all hilltop structures as essentially military. There are of course other ways of interpreting the material evidence. In terms of trying to understand the figure of Arthur, there are other reasons that can be put forward as to why he was fighting the Picts, Scots and Angles.

Chapter Three

Stories and Locations

ALTHOUGH WE HAVE VERY little material surviving from an early date in Scotland we are fortunate that a considerable amount of traditional material from Wales and Ireland has survived. In particular the Welsh traditional material surviving in such collections as *The Mabinogion* and the *Welsh Triads* has a great deal to tell us of how Arthur was perceived within ancient Welsh society. Such perceptions are likely to have been shared with the P-Celtic-speaking peoples who inhabited the southern part of Scotland, and possibly by the Picts. In *A Midsummer Eve's Dream* (p. 29), A. D. Hope tells us:

> With the coming of Christianity the religions and cults which it displaced did not simply disappear. The Divine beings were sometimes euhemerised into kings, queens and heroes of legendary history as happened in the sagas of pre-Christian Ireland. In other cases they were assimilated to historical or semi-historical persons, as some scholars suppose was the case with King Arthur and a Celtic god of the same name in Welsh tradition.

This would appear to make a great deal of sense, though in referring to Welsh tradition Hope may not have been thinking of the geographical extent in which the predecessor of the Welsh language was spoken. Earlier I mentioned W. F. Skene's suggestion that the stories of Arthur amongst the Britons and the story of Finn MacCoul among the Gaels might have originated from a very old common source in the area where these two different groups lived alongside each other. This brings us to the consideration of whether Arthur was essentially a mythological being or a historical warrior chief of the sixth century. The sources leading us to see him as essentially mythological are the works of Taliesin, the tales of *The Mabinogion* and other originally orally transmitted material such as the *Welsh Triads*. The reference to him in *The Gododdin* could be to either a mythical or a famous historical figure within contemporary society. Both mythology and legend arise from and through oral transmission. Literate society has very clear and precise ideas – we have dictionaries, encyclopaedias, glossaries and a vast array of other books that define the words and ideas we use. In pre-literate societies there are no such reference works and to some extent we can see that the stories through which belief and practice are passed on contain a totality of knowledge and information of central importance within such societies. They are part of a total belief culture which is not fixed in the sense that we see ideas and words. In one sense mythology is like poetry – it seeks to express the inexpressible and to understand the contradictions inherent in life itself. However, when one considers the actual process of transmitting ideas in pre-literate societies it becomes clear that the distinction between oral and literary material is not clear cut at all. The function of story within pre-literate societies is in many ways like history in a modern nation state. History attempts to give a clear common understanding of who we are and where we have come from. It gives a shared perception of our place in the world. However, history is subject to the old cliché of 'he who pays the piper calls the tune'. The particular message of any history is effectively decided by whoever controls society. In Scottish terms this has meant that we have been subjected to a primarily English version of the past, masquerading as British history. Saying this is not anti-English as many of the proponents of this version of history have been Scots who were more than happy to go along with this process. As noted, different societies can present totally different versions of the same events – one man's terrorist is often another's hero – meaning that history is rarely definitive.

In oral societies the situation is complicated by the actual function of oral transmission. One of Scotland's Arthurian stories makes this point. The story of Arthur and Vanora (Guinevere) from Meigle in Strathmore, a few miles north-east of Perth, tells of how the Queen betrayed Arthur by entering into a relationship with the Pictish Prince Modred when her husband set off on a pilgrimage to Rome. She ends up by being torn to death by a pack of wild hounds as punishment for her betrayal of both her husband and apparently the tribe, nation or society. In a pre-literate situation, where all moral precepts, all history, all genealogy, all lore and knowledge has to be passed on by word of mouth, the story of Arthur and Vanora has a function as a moral parable, illustrating the destructive results of adultery, particularly within a close-knit and inter-related society. In such a situation what matters is what works. With no definitive written history to fall back on, and despite the conservative tendencies of all storytellers to resist major tampering with tales, the situation can arise where a story might be made more effective by a reference to a recent historical event or personage. If the effectiveness of a story would be improved in such a way, by making it more memorable, it would indeed make sense to change it. Such a process would allow the distinction between mythological and legendary characters to become blurred over time. Given that the mindset of both story-teller and audience would be focussed on their family group or tribe, the idea that there could be an external, 'objective' reality which would deny the possibility of this being allowed to happen would simply not exist.

As Hope suggests, there have been many commentators on Arthurian material who see Arthur as having originated in the very far past as a god, and there are others who see him as essentially having been an actual sixth-century warrior Briton. The truth of the matter might be that he was both. Both Edward I of England and Robert I of Scotland deliberately evoked the Arthurian concept of uniting Britain to justify their own actions. With Edward it was the unification of the British Isles under English (his) rule, while Robert (the Bruce) used the idea of uniting the old tribal nations when he sent his brother to try and raise the Irish against Edward. Myth and legend do not only have political power within non-literate societies.

It is also a known process whereby a leader takes the name or title of some particularly famous tribal ancestor in order to boost his own importance and make him more attractive to his peers. This is also probably the reason why dynasties name succeeding sons after their fathers – a continuity of influence and power is suggested and supported. The reference to Arthur in *The Gododdin* suggests he could easily have been the subject of this type of process, the name of Arthur being synonymous with great valour and skill in battle. The reference shows that the intended audience knew exactly what, and who, was being referred to. In this sense Arthur is clearly the warrior par excellence. It is feasible there was a considerable corpus of tales concerning him and some of these might well have become incorporated into *The Mabinogion* and the poems of Taliesin. We do not know what stories of Arthur were told among the Gododdin themselves but in the surviving Arthurian material in Welsh we can perhaps find much the same tales. As we shall see, there are those who consider Artair, son of Aedan Mac Gabhran of Strathclyde, as the true and original Arthur, though he was born considerably later than most evidence suggests.

Because we know of the close contact between Picts and Scots and Britons and Scots it is worth considering whether Artair mac Aedan was in fact named by his Scottish father after a renowned hero amongst his neighbours. Given the location we shall consider for the supposedly historical battles of Arthur, the Scots of Dalriada would certainly have known of him. We do not know a great deal of how Christian the Dalriadan Scots were before the arrival of St Columba in 563 AD, but if Arthur was essentially fighting on behalf of the new religion, as the evidence strongly suggests, he would be a heroic figure in Columba's eyes. As Columba put Aedan on the throne of Dalriada, or perhaps ensured his chieftaincy, the naming of his son after a recent Christian hero would have perhaps made sense to Aedan.

Arthurian Place Names

The suggestion that Arthurian place names in Scotland are mainly a result of romantic influence by Malory and later authors on Scottish landowners who renamed some of their properties has never been proven. Nor is it ever likely to be. Just as there are place names associated with Finn MacCoul all over the once Gaelic-speaking areas of Scotland and Ireland, so we have Arthurian place names in different parts of Scotland where P-Celtic languages were spoken. We have already looked at the process by which this happened, but the telling of stories in particular environments to make them more effective does not help us understand whether the Arthur of Ben Arthur, Arthur's Seat and elsewhere was a mythological or historical character. It is relatively common throughout the world for the names of significant geographical locations to be named after mythological beings. If the process allowed the naming of a hill for a contemporary hero, place names would surely be subject to considerable change and would thus lose one of their most meaningful attributes – that the audience knows where exactly where you mean. It is also the case that most heroes would only be considered notable within their own tribe, even if their reputation was widespread amongst other tribes – though in this respect the historical Arthur would seem to be an exception. The reputation of such a hero would rely on his exploits against other tribes who would have little reason to honour him by naming some prominent landmark after him. One possibility does exist, however, in the case of alliances. If a particular hero came to the fore in one of the alliances we have considered, this might mean that he would have a reputation amongst all of those who accepted his leadership. There is no doubt that there are place names that have are associated with specific historical figures – there are innumerable Wallace's and Prince Charlie's caves in Scotland, some of which have changed from the former to the latter. Probably in a similar fashion Arthur became linked to some prehistoric monuments, which current understanding suggests must have happened long after these monuments were created. I am unaware of this process having been applied to any landmark as prominent as a mountain. Ben Arthur and Benartney might, of course, be the exceptions. We should remember that in sixth-century Scotland, and for a long time after, the majority of the population lived in small scattered family groups and were much more aware of their physical environment than city dwellers tend to be, and would naturally have a much more intimate relationship with it. The passing on of poems, stories and other lore described as happening within the known environment would have taken place within the kin group, giving it a directness and immediacy that modern history cannot have.

ARTHUR AT MEIGLE

The story of Arthur and Vanora at Meigle, north-east of Perth in Strathmore, is supported by a few local names: Arthurstone itself – there were two great standing stones nearby called Arthur's and Vanora's stones but only one survives; Arthurbank is a nearby farm and Arthur's Fold was the name of another. Additionally there is a local legend about Vanora's Stone, the majestic Pictish cross-slab (Meigle No. 4) in Meigle Museum, and Vanora's Mound in Meigle kirkyard. Because of her adultery and betrayal she was sentenced to be torn to death by wild dogs; this is how the locals interpreted the scene on the cross-slab on the other side from the cross. It shows a gowned figure surrounded by heavily shouldered animals, and in the official guide book it is said to be a representation of Daniel in the lions' den. It is an intriguing thought that it might have been interpreted in such divergent ways by different groups. In the kirkyard there is Vanora's Mound where her dismembered body is said to have been interred, with curses and imprecations heaped upon it. Such was the power of these curses that locals believed any woman foolish enough to stand on Vanora's Mound would be made sterile. Just as Arthur has been seen as supernatural so Vanora has been considered as some sort of fay, or fairy, and in this story the normal attributes of what might be a faded goddess figure have been transformed. A few miles away near Kirkmichael there is a stone known as Clach-na-Ban, the Woman's or Women's Stone, in the hollow of which young women would sit when wishing to become pregnant. The exact reversal of this well known and quite common type of practice in Meigle kirkyard is remarkable. It is tempting to see this story as some sort of Christian reworking of the original tale, particularly given some of the possibilities that would arise if Vanora was herself the embodiment of sovereignty. We shall look at the idea of female sovereignty later. The Iron Age hill fort on nearby Barry Hill where Vanora was imprisoned before her grisly execution was known locally as Modred's Castle. As we have seen, the fact that the Picts, like the Britons and the Gododdin, were P-Celtic-speaking it is likely that they had the same general mythological and legendary traditions as their neighbours. While language is an unsound basis on which to consider ethnicity it is the norm for people speaking the same or closely related languages to have the same mythological and religious beliefs, beliefs that were passed down by word of mouth, generation to generation.

All the stones in the collection of Pictish Symbol Stones at Meigle came from close by and indicate an early Christian site of some importance. It is likely that, as elsewhere, this was preceded by a pagan site at the same location. There are many Pictish

Symbol Stones which are clearly pagan on one side and Christian on the other, the crosses on the Christian side assumed to be later than the pagan symbols on the other. This might just be part of the standard Christian practice of re-using pagan sites, but I have suggested this would allow the stones to be used in delivering the message of both religions, suggesting perhaps a period when paganism and Christianity were co-existent within Pictish society. Just as motifs on the cross-slabs taken from the Bible were probably used to illustrate specific Bible texts, the symbols on the pagan sides could have had a similar function for a pagan audience. The later Pictish cross-slabs often have portrayals of the deer hunt and it has been suggested that this a reference to the eventual destruction or suppression of the old religion.

THE CASTLE OF MAIDENS

Many of the romances inspired by the spread of Arthurian tales by Breton troubadours and others after the Norman invasion of England in 1066 mention the Castle of the Maidens. It crops up in different early material too, as in the story of Peredur Longspear in *The Mabinogion*. The term Castle of the Maidens is the name given to Edinburgh in a series of historic documents from the twelfth and thirteenth centuries. It is in fact the normal name for Edinburgh in such documents for this period. It is an unfortunate fact of Scottish historiography that, due mainly to the fact that so many of our earlier records were destroyed by Southron invaders, our own historians, becoming accustomed to consulting external original sources, seem to have come to the conclusion that nothing original happened in Scotland. Everything that happened or developed here had to be explained by external influence. However, the term Castle of the Maidens is admirably suited to Castle Hill in Edinburgh. As I have shown in *The Quest for the Nine Maidens*, Edinburgh Castle Rock was associated with the putative early

Christian saint St Monenna who was associated with nine maidens, or more precisely eight virgins and a widow. There were many groups of nine maidens in Scotland and elsewhere (most of them obviously pagan), enough of them to suggest that the idea of such groups was widespread. Many were associated with hill or mountain tops, and some with islands. Skene claimed an early Welsh name for Castle Rock, Mynydd Agnedd, which he translated as Castle or Mount of the Maidens. There are records of there being a tradition in twelfth-century Edinburgh that the Castle was known as Castrum Puellarum, the Castle of the Maidens, because this was where the Picts kept their daughters. An early seal of Edinburgh shows maidens, three not nine, on the battlements of the castle. All of this I suggest shows the early provenance of the term for Edinburgh Castle Rock. J. Grant in *Old and New Edinburgh* (1 p. 15) tells us of St Monenna:

> The site of her edifice is supposed to be that now occupied by the Chapel of St Margaret, the most ancient piece of masonry in the Scottish capital; and it is a curious circumstance, with special reference to the fable of the Pictish princesses, that close by it, as recorded in *The Caledonian Mercury* of 20 September 1853, when some excavations were made, a number of human bones, apparently all females, together with some coffins, were found.

There was also a story that there had been a nunnery here but no records of one exist. The nunnery was said to have been replaced by a monastery as it was not fitting for the nuns to be around soldiers. If the female bodies were not nuns then could they have been the pagan priestesses I suggest? If so, this would be a fair reason for calling the site the Castle of Maidens. It is significant that many of the sites called Maiden Castle in Scotland and elsewhere in Britain are clearly not defensive and A. D. Hope in *A Midsummer Eve's Dream* (pp. 35f.) suggests the widespread occurrence of the Maidens motif in place names, ancient monuments and in harvest folk rituals was a remnant of an ancient cult, quite clearly pagan.

In the case of Edinburgh this seems to have combined with the political and military significance of the site in such a way as to give rise to it eventually becoming the capital of Scotland as a whole.

TRAPRAIN LAW

St Monenna is said also to have had a foundation on Traprain Law in East Lothian which also can be seen as a potential Castle of Maidens site. This was also the site where Geoffrey of Monmouth, and later romancers, located King Lot of the Lothians, who was married to Arthur's sister. Thenew, daughter of Lot, was cast adrift in an oarless boat after having been seduced, made pregnant and refusing to marry either her seducer or a shepherd. This is supposed to be because she had become a Christian and wanted to dedicate her life to Christ. She went on to give birth to St Kentigern, the supposed contemporary of St Columba and in whose story we first come across the figure later developed into Merlin, the wizard companion of King Arthur. Some of the miracles accorded to St Kentigern – bringing a dead man back to life, creating fire with his breath, and raising the river Forth in storm – seem to belong as much to pagan tradition as Christian. Kentigern was closely associated with Strathclyde, an area which was the source of much Arthurian material that survives in Welsh. Within the traditions we are considering it is significant that Traprain Law, earlier known as Dunpeldur, from the P-Celtic *paladyr* meaning spear shaft, was one of the significant settlements of the tribe the Romans called the Votadini, whom we know later as the Gododdin. The finding of a hoard of Roman silver on Traprain Law has led to all sorts of suggestions of a client relationship with the Romans, though its significance has been greatly exaggerated. The Antonine Wall either cut through the northern territory of the Votadini or was on the northern edge of it and we should remember that the raids carried out on Hadrian's Wall throughout the fourth century, and earlier, came mainly through their territory. If they had traditional relationships with the other tribal groupings of Scotland – the Britons of Strathclyde, the Picts and the Scots – it is difficult to understand why they would want to get too close to the Romans. This would mean offending their neighbours and apparently traditional allies. Again, our understanding of this is limited by the scarcity of early written materials and also, I suggest, by a failure of historians to realise that the behaviour of tribal societies is only in the most superficial sense like that of feudal societies. N. Chadwick in *The British Heroic Age* mentions that an excavation by A. O. Curle in 1914 and 1919 found evidence of occupation from the Stone Age to the fifth century but no evidence of Roman occupation of the hilltop site.

That there is stability within such societies is apparent from the fact that the tribal Votadini whom the Romans encountered were still in existence half a millennium later. Both Traprain Law and Edinburgh Castle were significant sites from an early period within their territory. King Loth of the Lothians was said to have been the father of both Modred and Gawain. Modred's role in Arthur's downfall is presented in some Scottish sources in a different fashion from Malory's idea of the adulterous usurper, just as Arthur is not presented universally as an infallible king. Gawain, of course, is central to the tale of Gawain and the Green Knight in which he is portrayed as a hero for accepting a Yuletide challenge from a supernatural giant. In this tale he agrees to subject himself to the fate he imposes on the Green Knight – beheading. After he beheads the Green Knight, the giant picks up his head and disappears saying he will return the following year. Being prepared to sacrifice himself because he had given his word, honour being integral to the concept of the tribal warrior, not just the fanciful knights of chivalry, he is spared. He proved himself worthy. This tale has been widely interpreted as a clouded reference to pagan practice possibly harking back to sacrifice at the winter solstice to ensure fertility for the coming year.

ARTHUR'S SEAT

The folklorist Donald A. Mackenzie in *Scottish Folk Lore and Folk Life* (p. 106) said there was a tale told of Arthur's Seat in Edinburgh that Arthur and his men were sleeping inside the hill, awaiting the call to come forth to the aid of Scotland. This is exactly the same tale told of the Eildon Hills overlooking Melrose in the Scottish Borders. The Eildon Hills, known to the Romans as Trimontium, are a very distinctive group of three peaks which are also associated with Thomas the Rhymer, the famous Scottish prophet who is said to have lived in the thirteenth century at nearby Earlston. He was carried off to the Otherworld by the Queen of Faerie where he was given the gift of second sight. This suggests an ongoing continuity of pagan belief associated with this site. Songs about Thomas are still being sung within folk tradition.

R. Hutton in his *Pagan Religion in Prehistoric Britain* made a suggestion I believe might be related to this belief about Arthur and his Sleeping Warriors, which is matched in places where Gaelic used to be spoken by similar tales of Finn and the Fianna. Writing of the significance of chambered tombs in Britain, now known to have been the sites of multiple partial burials rather than the burials of great aristocrats that earlier historians preferred, he makes some intriguing suggestions. Many of the excavated chambered tombs show a pattern of containing only the skulls and thigh bones of numerous individuals and of having been opened upon an annual basis. Hutton suggests that some sort of ceremony to contact the ancestors was carried out, probably at the end of autumn at a date corresponding to the modern Halloween, after the harvest was in and new crops planted. This is the time in traditional belief when the boundaries between this world and the next were at their weakest and when all sorts of shades and spirits walked the earth. It was also the best time to try and speak to the ancestors – when their spirits were nearest to us. Hutton suggests that the thigh bones and skulls, the largest bones, were brought out of the tombs to be used in a direct attempt to entreat the ancestors to work their magic on the planted crops to ensure fertility in the coming year, after the winter. After all, had the ancestors not returned to the earth, ashes to ashes, dust to dust? The retention of the skulls and the largest bones was perhaps seen as a way of keeping in touch in the right circumstances. This seems to me to be a suitable origin for both the idea of the Sleeping Warriors and the widespread motif of the fairy fiddlers where musicians are lured into fairy hills to play overnight for dancing. When they come out in the morning they find many years have passed. The association of Arthur with this motif represents an ongoing continuity of pagan belief. It seems that within the kin-group or tribe the ancestors, though on a different plane, were still considered to be part of a shared universe. Both Arthur and Finn MacCoul in Q-Celtic-speaking areas became associated with chambered tombs and stone circles, again suggesting some sort of continuity of pagan ideas with specific locations.

The recurrence of the motif of the Castle of Maidens in Arthurian romance strongly suggests that it was an integral part of the original oral tales associated with Arthur, and if Edinburgh was an original Castle of the Maidens then this further underlines the provenance of Arthur as a mythological figure among the P-Celtic-speaking tribes of north Britain. Edinburgh was a capital of the Gododdin, who definitely knew of Arthur. This, I would suggest, makes Arthur's Seat a credible Arthurian location. Before deserting the maidens it is worth noting that this motif of the Nine Maidens crops up significantly in Arthurian tales. In *Vita Merlini* Geoffrey of Monmouth tells us that after the fateful Battle of Camlaan, Arthur was taken off to the magic Isle of Avalon by Morgan, and eight sisters, of whom she was the leader. They were known for their healing powers and lived on Avalon, a name perhaps meaning the Island of Apples and which is clearly an

Otherworld island. It is usually interpreted as a Celtic paradise island and Markale in *Women of the Celts* (p. 285) tells us: 'Morgan's kingdom is the Isle of Avalon, the mythical isle somewhere in the sea, the island in the middle of the world, a kind of navel but also a matrix, an inexhaustible store of energy. There Arthur stays until he can be reborn and return to the world. There Queen Morgan reigns . . .' Morgan is clearly developed from an earlier goddess figure and may be linked to the Irish Morrigan, a battle goddess. Other commentators have suggested a similarity with the Norse Valhalla, the warriors' paradise and the link to a battle goddess, and the fact that the Norse Valkyries were often presented as nine in number would support this. In the poem *Priddeu Annwn* attributed to the semi-mythical Welsh poet Taliesin, Arthur leads a raid on the Underworld where the cauldron of the Welsh goddess Cerridwen is kept, tended by nine maidens. This is the Cauldron of Poetry and Inspiration and we seem to be deep in myth here. There are those who see this poem not as mythological but as a mystical representation of an actual raid, as we shall see. Elsewhere, in the *Mabinogion* tale *Peredur son of Efrawg*, the hero is given arms and training by the Nine Witches of Caer Llyow whom he eventually has to fight and defeat. These different groups of Nine Maidens could hardly be closer to the heart of Arthurian tradition and they themselves are but a part of a continuum of pre-Christian belief that covers several continents and can be seen as stretching back to Magdelanian times, between 10,000 and 15,000 BC in Iberia. If my contention regarding the telling of mythic and legendary material within the known environment of the tribe or society is correct, there is a prime candidate for Avalon in the River Forth. This is the Island of May, a Scots word meaning maiden, which has been archaeologically proved to have been both a pre-Christian and a Christian sacred site. Could this have been presented as Avalon in the traditional myths and legends of the Gododdin? Through the story of

Thenew, mother of St Kentigern, this island is linked to Traprain Law, and Culross on the north shore of the Forth, a noted early Christian site. J. S. Glennie suggested that Thenew might have been one of Monenna's nine maidens, underlining the fact that Arthur is surrounded by figures who belong as much to pagan tradition as to Christian belief, even in later works like Malory's *Morte d'Arthur*.

DUMBARTON ROCK

There are several traditions connecting Arthur with Dumbarton Rock, the great cleft rock commanding the north bank of the River Clyde, a few miles west of Glasgow. The Welsh *Bruts*, a collection of early traditional material, say that one of Arthur's battles was at Alclud, the ancient name for Dumbarton meaning the Height on the Forth, a good description. Skene placed the battle Nennius says was fought at Kaerlium at Dumbarton. In a charter of 1367 Dumbarton is recorded as 'Castrum Arthuri' which suggests a local tradition having given rise to the name. J. S. Glennie (p. 88) mentions a local tradition that Modred was born here. Dumbarton itself may have been used by the Romans; it was a handy defensive site controlling the Clyde near to the western end of the Antonine Wall and as such would have been ideal for supplying the garrison of the western section of the wall by water. The Romans, like the natives before them, would have been well aware of the relative speed of water communication as opposed to travel over land in boggy, heavily wooded Scotland. This was another site associated with St Monenna and her Nine Maidens, which suggests a continuity of some sacral significance from pagan times. It is noticeable, from a certain angle to the south east, that the cleft rock of Dumbarton bears some resemblance to a pair of female breasts. In Scotland there are several breast-shaped hills and mountains, called *pap* in Scots and *cioch* in Gaelic, that have ancient stories and prehistoric monuments associated with them. Their shapes could have been regarded as significant in a religion that worshipped an all-embracing mother goddess, which does seems to have been the earliest form of religion in Scotland as elsewhere. One such prominent hill is Bennachie in Aberdeenshire, originally Beinn a Cioch, the hill of the paps or nipples. It has several ancient structures on it, linked tales of giants and the Devil, nearby stone circles and at one time on its southern slope near the summit, Arthourscairne. Again we have the link between an Arthurian place name and a site of apparent ancient sanctity. St Monenna is also connected with Edinburgh Castle Rock, Traprain Law and Stirling Castle Rock. These sites thus appear to have been pre-Christian sacred sites, a fact overlooked in the military analysis to which hilltop sites have usually been subjected. It can hardly be coincidental that we have Arthurian associations with these sites.

There is a tradition amongst the Campbells, long one of Scotland's dominant clans and subsequently powerful aristocrats, that they are descended from a son of 'king' Arthur, called Smervie Mor, and that he was born on the south side of Dumbarton Rock in the Tower of the Red Hall. I. M. M. MacPhail in his book *Dumbarton Castle* (p. 3) tells us that there was a Red Tower on Dumbarton Rock that was repaired in 1460. He also refers to an old Gaelic rhyme about the Galbraiths, an old British name, that says, in translation, 'Briton of the Red Hall/Your name's the noblest race in Scotland.' We will look at the Campbell and MacArthur traditions later. Dumbarton Rock is generally thought to be the location of a story from *Life of Kentigern* in which he comes to the aid of the queen. Dumbarton is accepted as the capital of Strathclyde and it is of some significance that it is on the northern shore of the Clyde. North of Dumbarton the British polity of Strathclyde abutted the Picts and to the west the Scots, and probably to the east the Gododdin. Where the borders between the various groups lay is still to be discovered. In an echo of the story of Arthur and Vanora, it seems the queen had been unfaithful with one of the king's warriors. Stupidly she gave him a ring that the king had given her. One day the king was walking along the banks of the River Clyde when he came upon the warrior fast asleep. He saw the ring on the warrior's little finger and recognised it. Carefully he drew the ring without waking him and threw it into the river. On returning to the court he asked the queen why she wasn't wearing the ring, and where it was. She claimed to have mislaid it and said she would find it, only to then learn that the warrior had lost the ring. Realising the king was aware of her betrayal she went to St Kentigern for help. He told her to get her servant to go and fish in the river. This was done and the maid caught a fine salmon which she brought to the queen and the saint. The saint then cut open the salmon's belly and there was the ring. The queen took it to the king who could no longer accuse her of adultery. This story is referred to in the City of Glasgow's coat of arms. It is also a very strange story in that here we have a Christian saint, great nephew of Arthur, helping a queen to avoid a charge of adultery of which she was guilty. Behind this there is obviously something older than the life of the saint, and in the saint's acceptance of the queen's adultery there is perhaps a faint echo of the idea of sovereignty personified in a queen, and thus possibly of a matrilineal dynastic system. Whatever the original idea behind this motif was, the story shows that much of our early Christian material in Scotland, as elsewhere, contains remnants of earlier beliefs.

BEN ARTHUR AND ARGYLL

In Argyll, close to if not within the bounds of Dalriada, there is the mountain called Ben Arthur. The naming of mountains after actual heroes is not something often encountered and this suggests a clear reference to a mythological being. Skene, however, suggests that the mountain was named in honour of Arthur after his victory in the battle which Nennius refers to as being on the River Douglas, though there is another possible location for this battle, as we shall see later. Ben Arthur overlooks Loch Long, the name of which means the Loch of the Ships, from the Gaelic *luing*, a boat, reminding us that sea travel was a regular occurrence in sixth-century Britain. If this battle did take place here, could it have been that this was an attempt to carry out a flanking attack on Dumbarton? This route would also lead to the area of the Lennox and thus towards the lands around Stirling, an area whose strategic importance saw it being the site of major battles up until the eighteenth century. In the immediate vicinity there is also Agaidh Artair, Arthur's Face, a distinctive rock in Glenkinglas, and at Glassary in Argyll Sruth Artair, Arthur's burn, or stream. These locations are within what is considered to have been the Q-Celtic-speaking area of Scotland in the sixth century. This could be because the name was older than the arrival of Q-Celtic speakers in the area, though this is hardly provable, or it could mean that Arthur was a heroic figure to all of the tribal peoples of Scotland at this time. There are echoes of Arthurian material in some traditional Gaelic stories. The story of Mac Iain Direach in volume one of J. F. Campbell's *Popular Tales of the West Highlands* has a magical sword, a quest and a group of seven giant women who might be akin to the nine maidens found in *The Mabinogion* and elsewhere. The seven women in the tale are known as the Seven Big Women of Jura and as we shall see there are grounds for seeing the Corryvreckan whirlpool off Jura's northern coast as being of considerable significance in pagan belief. There are several other tales of female groups on Scottish islands who clearly derive from pre-Christian sources.

In this respect it is worth remembering that travel by sea from the Inner Hebrides to elsewhere in Scotland and to Wales and

Brittany was commonplace. The centre of Dalriada was the hill fort at Dunadd. This is in the Kilmartin valley, an area heavily clustered with ancient monuments that speak of a continuum of pre-Christian sanctity in this area stretching back to Megalithic times. The Kilmartin valley is easily accessible by sea from the Inner Hebrides and beyond, and is only a few sea-miles from the Corryvreckan whirlpool. There is mention in Adomnan's *Life of St Columba* of a trading ship arriving here from Gaul, underlining the continuity of sea travel. Perhaps too much attention has been paid in the past to the fact that the people of Dalriada and Strathclyde, Manau Gododdin, Wales and so on spoke separate languages. The languages are distinct but related, and we cannot state that the sixth-century tribal peoples of Britain were all mono-linguistic. Their proximity to each other, their similar economies and lifestyles suggests they had much in common.

BENARTNEY HILL

Another suggested Arthurian place name is Benartney overlooking Loch Leven in Fife. This hill has the outline of a sleeping giant, a hill fort and several wells. There are also the remains of what seems a once massive wall, and a place name Navitie Hill which is thought to derive from Nemeton, meaning a sacred enclosure. The cluster of possible pagan referents suggests an ancient sanctity, an idea strengthened by the island in the loch below which is called St Serf's Island. St Serf was an early saint who killed dragons, usually a metaphor for defeating paganism, and was a Culdee. The Culdees were the descendants of the original Columban church who continued to officiate in several Scottish cathedrals for centuries after the Synod of Whitby in 664 which effectively installed the superiority of Rome. When Thenew came ashore at Culross to give birth to St Kentigern they were both taken in by St Serf who became Kentigern's tutor, which links him to Arthur. There is a fascinating eye-witness account of a Beltane (May 1) ceremony at the Dragon's Cave on Kinnoull Hill, Perth, from 1559. This ceremony was said to be in honour of St Serf's victory over a dragon and seems to be much more pagan than Christian, though it survived within the Christian population. If Benartney is indeed an Arthurian place-name it can be seen as underlining the continuum between pagan and Christian. The sleeping giant of Benartney Hill is not referred to as Arthur and might be better interpreted as a goddess figure.

DOLLAR

In the county of Clackmannan – the name perhaps originating from the name of the stone in the centre of the village of Kincardine, Clach Manau, which perhaps relates to the lands of Manau Gododdin – there is another village called Dollar. This has been the subject of some speculation as to whether it might relate to Castle Dolour which occurs in the early Welsh tale of Peredur Longspear, and elsewhere in later Arthurian romance. Received opinion, sure that Arthur originated south of the border between England and Scotland, has dismissed this as nonsense, or perhaps another instance of a name arising from literature. Dollar is situated not far from the Forth at the foot of the Ochil hills, a P-Celtic name meaning high ground. Above the village at the head of a striking cleft is Castle Campbell, a late medieval Scottish castle. Its striking location gives it a remarkable view over the Forth valley, where there are several potential sites for Arthur's battles according to Nennius. In the hills behind the castle there are several ancient sites, wells and intriguing place names redolent of paganism, including a Maidens Well. There are two streams called the Burn of Sorrow and the Burn of Care. There is a fifteenth-century papal bull which refers to the place as Castle Gloum. However, the most remarkable aspect of Castle Campbell is its precise location. In his book *Paganism in Arthurian Romance* J. Darrah gives a description of Castle Dolour, or Dolorous Gard, taken from the thirteenth-century Arthurian text the *Vulgate Merlin Continuation*:

> It was situated high on a native rock. At its foot ran the river 'Hombre' on one side and on the other a large river which came from more than forty springs which poured through an arch at the base of the 'tower'. Within the 'keep' was what seems from the description to have been a chambered barrow later opened and re-used. (Darrah, p. 198)

Castle Campbell has a stream running past it on the east which is met just below the large outcrop of rock on which it stands. This stream is met by another rushing through a gorge which is fed from a host of small springs on the hill above the castle. Although there is no arch over the top of the dramatic cleft now, it looks like there may well have been one in the past. The description is very close, though place name scholars see the name as coming from the Welsh *dol* or Gaelic *dul*, meaning valley, presumably referring to the lands around the village. Is it possible that this was the origin of Castle Dolour in *The Mabinogion*? Darrah, seeing Arthurian material as only present in the Welsh landscape, says of the description, 'Perhaps it will enable someone to locate the place somewhere in the Severn.' As we have seen, there are Arthurian traditions at several locations in Scotland and certainly in the Forth valley.

The Scottish place name specialist W. J. Watson in *Celtic Place Names in Scotland* also mentions an Arthurseat in Aberdeen and a Suidhe Artair in Glenlivet in Banffshire, and Glennie mentions an Arthur's Seat north-east of Forfar. These locations strengthen the notion that Arthur was known amongst the Pictish tribes. It is an intriguing thought that as there are several words used in place names in Welsh and Gaelic that mean the same and are similar in sound, for example Glynn and Glen, Lynn and Linn, Moal and Moel, many Scottish place names may still contain names that originated in early P-Celtic forms. Our maps have all been created since P-Celtic disappeared from Scotland and many such names have consequently been Gaelicised. Does this mean that there are areas of Scotland wrongly assumed to have once been Gaelic-speaking? Other than the Arthurian place names in Argyll, which was Gaelic-speaking in the sixth century, and the story of Mac Iain Direach, I am unaware of any extensive Scottish Gaelic material preceding the well known ballad *Am Bron Binn*, several versions of which were collected from Gaelic singers in the late nineteenth century. As with much other material passed through oral tradition we do not know how old this ballad might be. There are, however, some Gaelic texts of Arthurian material I have not been able to find in translation, though most scholars see them as being late and based upon material from outside Scotland.

STIRLING

Just below the rock on which Stirling Castle stands, between it and the River Forth, there is an unusual circular-shaped earthwork, known as the King's Knot, which has been associated with King Arthur since medieval times and has been suggested as the Round Table itself. The Round Table was not invented until the twelfth century but there are other interesting links in the area. This was the part of Scotland where invading armies would often come to battle with the natives. The line of the Antonine Wall is only a few miles to the south and Dumyat, the fort of the Miathi, is close by. The *Annals of Ulster* mention the battle between them and Aedan Mac Gabhran as the battle of Mannan or Manau in the year 582. It was this battle that saw the death of Artair, son of Aedan of Strathclyde, who is considered by sòme to have been the historical Arthur. William Wallace and Robert the Bruce both fought invading English armies here and as late as the seventeenth and eighteenth centuries there were battles here between various forces. The pass between the Kilsyth Hills and the Ochil Hills is the natural route for anyone heading north in Scotland, and the pass is effectively controlled by Stirling Castle. This was another site associated with the supposed early Christian saint Monenna. Robert the Bruce gained his famous victory at nearby Bannockburn in 1314. In the tale of *Culhwch and Olwen*, mention is made of two magical oxen Nyniaw and Peibiaw who had initially been men but due to their sinful behaviour had been turned into beasts by God. One of them is said to have been from beyond Mynydd Bannawg, which has been suggested (G. and T. Jones, p. 96) as part of the Grampian Mountains. It is more likely to have been the range of hills west of Stirling that includes the Kilsyth Hills and the Campsie Fells, where the Bannock Burn rises, an identification that W. J. Watson was happy with (W. J. Watson, p. 196). In one medieval romance Lancelot's father is said to have held the lands of Benois which may be a variation of Bannock. Nyniaw and Peibiaw have been identified by John MacQueen with St Ninian and his companion Plebia (MacQueen, p. 76). In *St Nynia*, MacQueen also mentions a *Life of St Cadoc*, believed to have been contemporary with the tale of *Culhwch and Olwen*, which mentions Cau of Prydyn who lived beyond Mount Bannog. There are grounds for considering Welsh references to Prydein or Prydyn as meaning the land of the Picts, north of the Kilsyth Hills. Could this be the Caw whose 19 sons, some of whom have Gaelic-sounding names, are in the list of Arthur's men in *Culhwch and Olwen*? In that tale we read of Gildas as the son of Cau. This suggests Gildas might originally have been a Pict, though his name is thought to be Gaelic, if indeed this refers to the Gildas who wrote *The Ruin of Britain*. The relationships between the various tribes and tribal confederations of Dark Age Britain were more fluid and intermingled than the analysis based on regarding them as discrete mono-linguistic kingdoms would have us believe. Just because the tales were written down does not mean they ceased being passed on orally and it might be that some of the writers creating later Arthurian material would have had some access to this type of material.

FALKIRK

Less than ten miles south and east of Stirling is Falkirk which has its own series of Arthurian associations. This is very close to the eastern end of the Antonine Wall and nearby on the north bank of the River Carron there used to be an ancient building locally called Arthur's O'on, or oven. It was demolished in the middle of the eighteenth century but there is little doubt that it was originally a Roman temple that had become associated with Arthur. Close by are the twin hills of Dunipace that Skene suggested as the site of the battle Nennius described as being on the river called Bassas. These great mounds have been suggested as essentially natural features but they appear too regular to be entirely natural. Another Bass, at Inverurie south of Aberdeen, is over 50 feet high and bears a close resemblance to the great mounds on which several Early Christian churches were raised, one fine example being St Vigeans at Arbroath, which is also the site of a noted collection of Pictish Symbol Stones. I do not think it stretching a point, given the deliberate re-usage of pagan sites by the Early Christian church, to suggest some ritual activity being associated with such mounds, whether or not they were wholly or partially artificial. Perhaps like some ancient burial mounds and notable hills, they were associated with the ideas of the ancestors we have seen in the traditions of Arthur sleeping with his warriors awaiting the call to arms, and the linked traditions of fiddlers lured in to fairy mounds to play music for the fairies to dance to.

Camelon, suggested as the site of the Battle of Camlaan, is now part of Falkirk. As we shall see when we consider the 12 battles attributed to Arthur by Nennius, the district on the south of the River Forth provides excellent locations for a number of these battles. Glennie (pp. 48f.) suggests this area was also the location of the Battle of Catraeth, the ill-fated battle of the poem *The Gododdin*. Close to the eastern end of the Antonine Wall extensive Roman remains have been mentioned by several authors, which may refer to the original site of the City of the Legions. The continuing association of Arthur with locations that are sites of pre-Christian sanctity makes sense in that there are repeated references to him battling pagan Picts, Saxons and Scots. Bellenden mentions that the Roman general Vespasian was based at Camelon.

The fact that we find Arthurian associations with a range of sites – Edinburgh Castle, Dumbarton Rock, Stirling Castle, Traprain Law – which I have identified as being Nine Maidens sites is intriguing particularly as the list of Arthur's battles as given by Nennius shows many of them to have been close to major pagan centres. This is not fortuitous and I hope to show that these battles could have been part of a concerted attack by Arthur, a Christian battle leader, against the forces of paganism. The idea of a warrior taking the name of a mythological ancestor or a mythical hero is distinctly possible and perhaps what we have in Arthur's attack on such sites is a warrior using such a procedure to attack the very belief system that gave rise to the practice itself. What cannot be doubted is that in the ongoing transmission of the Arthurian material in Scotland and Wales, in Brittany and subsequently throughout much of north-western Europe, in ensuing centuries there is a tale that had a powerful hold in the popular imagination. Stories only survive because either people want to hear them, or they say something that people need to hear. In this sense the moral aspects of much of the original Arthurian material can be seen as part of the very psychological binding of tribal society in P-Celtic-speaking areas. The later spread might be precisely because he was a suitable hero for the ongoing Christianisation of Europe. After all, it wasn't until after the year 1000 that all of Scandinavia became Christianised and rituals that were essentially pagan continued until very recently. The significance of the reference to Arthur in *The Gododdin* is that the audience would know who he was. Given that the poem is now thought to have been written towards the close of the sixth century it is feasible that the reference is to an actual warrior-hero of a couple of generations before. The extent of the place names associated with him covers a considerable part of Scotland and, as we have seen, includes areas occupied by both P- and Q-Celtic-speaking peoples.

We know that Christianity was being actively propagated by the Columban church in the second half of the sixth century and the Battle of Arfderydd in 573, in which Merlin supposedly went mad, is presented as an absolute Christian triumph over paganism. The process by which heroes could take the place of gods or supernatural beings in tales could provide a model for Christian monks wanting to tell the best story they could. Just as the storyteller in the tribe was answerable to the needs of the tribe, so the churchman was answerable to the needs of the church. Would some of these churchmen, raised in the tribe and subsequently educated in the church, have had divided loyalties when traditional beliefs clashed with their religious training? Is this why we can still see so much that clearly derives from paganism in the early material from both Wales and Ireland?

There are other Arthur place names in Scotland which may relate to our hero: Arthurlie in Glasgow, Arthurbridge in Moray and many others. If his provenance in Scotland, or even within the oral culture of the P-Celtic-speaking peoples of post-Roman Scotland, is accepted then this should hardly surprise us. J. S. Glennie in *Arthurian Localities in Scotland* gives an extensive list of names that occur in the surviving Welsh sources, matched to Scottish locations. John Randall in *Arthur and Merlin: The Tweeddale Connection* (p. 11) made a possibly telling point when he noted that the section of Nennius's History dealing with Arthur is alongside his treatment of the Northern History and the battles with the Anglians of Northumbria.

Chapter Four

The Early Sources

THE EARLIEST REFERENCE TO Arthur was, as we have seen, in the poem *Y Gododdin*, which, it has been suggested, was composed in the latter years of the sixth century, some 50 or 60 years after Arthur is said to have died in the Battle of Camlaan. As a work of heroic poetry it has been seen as being of secondary importance to annals and other historical documents. Such documentation, particularly when unsupported, also requires to be treated with caution. There were no written narrative histories at this time and we are forced to rely on contemporary or near contemporary records that are quite clearly propagandist, driven by religious rather than historical requirements, or that arise from incidental entries in annals. Annals were kept in monasteries initially to help calculate moveable dates in the Christian calendar and over time entries of significant events began to be entered in their margins. While this means that such entries are not meant to carry a historical narrative, it also means that they are not being manipulated in a propagandist fashion, at least in their original forms. Later copies of them, which is what we have to rely on for all of the earliest sources, might have been subject to manipulation. However, we have no means of knowing exactly how information reached the various monasteries from which annals have survived. Before the triumph of the Roman faction at the Synod of Whitby in 664 AD we can surmise that the Columban monasteries were more closely linked to their local communities than they subsequently became. This might have meant a greater sympathy to traditional material in the earlier years of Christianity in north Britain.

GILDAS

The only extensive work we have from sixth-century Britain is Gildas's *The Ruin of Britain*. The purpose of this work, which is little more than a religious polemic, was to explain the sins and calamities of the Britons that had led them to being subject to raiding by the Picts and Scots. He contrasts the troubled present with the peace and prosperity of Roman rule which had ended before his birth. We know from Roman sources such as Ammianus Marcellinus that in fact the Picts and Scots had been raiding the Roman provinces jointly since at least the fourth century, sometimes in alliance with Saxons. Given the propensity for raiding within warrior society, and the fact that the Romans had invaded the northern parts of Britain on several occasions, this was hardly to be wondered at. Due to the influence of classical education many historians have been eager to present the invasion of northern Britain by Romans as some sort of benefit to the natives. Sure they might be subjugated, their warriors might be slaughtered and their social system destroyed but what was that against the benefits of Roman rule? This raiding, according to Gildas, had led to the hiring of Saxon mercenaries from the Continent, who then turned against the Britons, becoming even more of a plague than the raiders from the north. He tells that resistance against these turncoats was led by one Ambrosius Aurelanius, who has been suggested as if not the original on whom Arthur was based at least a predecessor in fighting off the invaders. We know, however, that the Angles had been allying with both Picts and Scots to raid the Romans centuries before this. A recurring interpretation has been that Aurelius and Arthur were attempting to restore something of the previous Roman order upon barbarian Britain. If I am right in suggesting that Arthur was mainly active in central Scotland, the idea of him trying to recreate a society that had disappeared southwards 300 years earlier, and had only been in occupation of some parts of Scotland for short periods, is frankly unsustainable. Even in England the Romans had been absent since the early years of the fifth century and to suggest that over a century later there was deliberate attempt to emulate Roman behaviour seems far-fetched. However, we should remember that the Christian church in the West developed out of the ruins of the Roman Empire and that the education of monks like Gildas was a combination of Biblical studies and Greek and Roman Classics.

Modern scholarship has shown that the idea of a major invasion by Germanic-speakers from the Low Countries has been vastly overstated. Troops recruited from the tribal peoples of the Low Countries and Germany had been part of the Roman armies since they first arrived and it was standard practice for veterans to settle in suitable country near where they had been stationed once they retired. The acquisition of a decent plot of land would have been an attractive recruiting tool. Modern interpretations see the settlement of English-speaking peoples in southern Britain as a long drawn-out process taking many centuries. However, from Gildas's point of view as someone drawing attention to the sins and improprieties of his contemporaries, the effectiveness of his argument did not rely on historical accuracy. *The Ruin of Britain* is essentially a moral tract and not an attempt at a history. Here is an example of his style:

Britain has kings, but they are tyrants: she has judges but they are wicked. They often plunder and terrorise – the innocent: they defend and protect – the guilty and thieving; they have many wives – whores and adulteresses; they constantly swear – false oaths; they make vows – but almost at once tell lies; they wage wars – civil and unjust; they chase thieves energetically all over the country – but love and even reward the thieves who sit with them at table; they distribute alms profusely – but pile up an immense mountain of crime for all to see; they take their seats as judges – but rarely seek out the rules of right judgement; they despise the harmless and humble; but exalt to the stars, so far as they can, their military companions, bloody, proud and murderous men, adulterers and enemies of God – if chance as they say, so allows: men who should have been rooted out vigorously, name and all; they keep many prisoners in their jails, who are most often loaded with chafing chains because of intrigue than because they deserve punishment. They hang around the altars swearing oaths – then shortly afterwards scorn them as though they were dirty stones. (p. 29)

Likewise his description of the Picts and Scots shows his attitude towards these barbarians when he calls them 'foul hordes of Scots and Picts, like dark throngs of worms who wriggle out of narrow fissures in the rock when the sun is high and the weather grows warm.' (p. 23) This is hardly the stuff of objective history! He tells that the Britons fought against the invaders under the leadership of Aurelius Ambrosius who he says was a Roman. This probably means of Roman descent. And he tells us that the struggle went on up to the Battle of Badon Hill when the natives were victorious. As later writers tell that Arthur fought at Badon Hill there has been some suggestion that Aurelius and Arthur were the same person, but Gildas does not specifically say that Aurelius fought at Badon Hill. He does say that he himself was born in the year of the Battle of Badon which is now thought to have taken place around 516. Gildas also tells us that there had been peace since the Battle of Badon Hill at which the invaders had been defeated. He then goes on to heap invective upon a group of contemporary kings for a variety of sins. Gildas's diatribe is anachronistic in our modern world but the historian John Morris noted that the growth of monasticism within the Christian church in Wales and Gaul was greatly influenced by him. It is thought that Gildas was born in Strathclyde but moved to south Wales, something that we have already seen was not unusual. The fact that he makes no specific mention of Arthur seems strange, but as he was based in Wales he might have had little interest in what was happening a couple of hundred miles to the north. If the historical Arthur had been primarily active in Wales one would perhaps expect Gildas to have made some mention of him.

Nowadays we know the immigration of Angles and Saxons into the British Isles took much longer and was more complex than was previously thought. From Gildas's point of view historical accuracy was secondary to his purpose in delivering a moral homily against the sins of his time, sins which, although he does not make it explicit, can be read as referring to pagan beliefs. He was certainly at pains to point out that none of the rulers he knew of were good Christians. He also paints a picture of a society which was anything but stable. However, in the figure of Aurelius Ambrosius as a leader of native Romanised Britons against incoming tribes from Europe we have a model that has been used to try to understand Arthur. It is a model that is attractive to those who have seen Roman influence as primary and have interpreted much of the history of the British Isles as arising from a series of military conquests. There had of course been a concerted invasion by the Romans, and when the Normans likewise invaded they saw Arthur as a suitable hero. Skene made the interesting point in *Arthur and the Britons in Scotland* (p. 15) that Gildas appeared to have been familiar with the geography of the area of north Somerset. Why then he did not identify the location of Badon Hill as being near Bath? The inference surely must be that he knew it to be elsewhere. In Bower's *Scotichronicon*, a fifteenth-century work of Scottish history, there is an interesting reference to Gildas (2 p. 59) when we are told: 'About this time died Gildas, a reliable and witty historian. He was buried in the old church on the island of Avalon . . . He stayed for a long time in that same island of Avalon for which he felt a strong affection and he delighted in the sanctity of that place.' This makes it clear that in Scotland as late as the fifteenth century the Isle of Avalon was considered to be an actual place and the surmise must be that Bower knew of the location to which he was referring. However, we should consider that as far as can be told Gildas, though possibly born in Strathclyde, spent most of his life in south Wales. It seems more than likely that

Bower was referring to Glastonbury, known through much of the Middle Ages as Avalon.

BEDE

Bede's *A History of the English Church and Peoples* has been extensively relied on by historians since he completed it around 730. The fact is that he makes no mention of Arthur, as a king or a war leader, but his history is hardly exhaustive and tellingly is a history of the English church and people. He does talk of Scotland but not in great detail. This can be interpreted as supportive of Arthur having been active in the north and thus to some extent outside what Bede considered his remit. The title is illustrative of his approach as he was a cleric at the monastery of Jarrow in Northumbria. By his time the consolidation of earlier social structures into kingdoms appears to have been well established and the Anglian kingdom of Northumbria had set out on an active policy of expansion and conquest in the previous century, at one time threatening to take control of most of northern Britain. This was the background against which Bede wrote and it creates some problems with his treatment of earlier times. It is from Bede that we inherit the division of the peoples of Britain by language groups. He says there were five languages in Britain: English, British, Scots, Pictish and Latin. Nowadays it is thought that despite what he wrote, Pictish was a language closely related to British, both of them being P-Celtic dialects. He also speaks of four nations: the English, British, Picts and Scots. His understanding of what life was like in tribal areas must have been limited as he had been brought up and educated within a Christian clerical establishment. Further to this, virtually all commentators on Bede have been happy to accept that by Scots he meant people from Ireland.

This depends on the idea of the Scots coming into Argyll on

the west coast of Scotland and setting up the 'kingdom' of Dalriada around 500 AD. In the light of modern archaeological investigation this idea is no longer tenable and it now appears that the Scots of Dalriada, as the area was then known, had in fact been settled there for centuries before this. Bede defines each of these peoples by their language and he was aware of the importance of the Columban church on Iona, the language of which was Gaelic, what he called Scots. In one of the ironies of history the language still extensively spoken in Scotland that was descended from the Northumbrian form of Anglo-Saxon is called Scots. English developed from the Mercian, and more Saxon, form of the language. Bede tells of the Christianisation of Northumbria under King Oswald in 635 and that this was led by Aidan, a monk who had come from Iona, the home of the Columban church. This tells us that substantial parts of northern Britain were still pagan at this time and that the main force of the Christian religion was the Columban church based on the west coast of Scotland. He also tells us that Aidan was not fluent in English when he came but that he was assisted by Oswald who had learned Gaelic while in exile in Iona. In Book 3, Chapter 2 (p. 139) Bede tells us: 'When King Oswald was about to give battle to the heathen, he set up the sign of the holy cross, and kneeling down, asked God that He would grant his heavenly aid to those who trusted in Him in their dire need.' This is explicit; the Christian leader is battling the heathen and this echoes the statements from Nennius and others that Arthur fought with the cross on his shield. While we have to be critical (after all Bede is a Christian monk writing a Christian history) there is a pattern here. The battle with the heathen is important, whether or not it could be used by this period as an excuse for expansion and conquest. Bede clearly sees contemporary Britain as being formed of kingdoms or nations each with its own distinctive language. As we have seen, in tribal areas such distinctions have little relevance. Historians have generally accepted this ethno-linguistic definition of nation states as the model for understanding not just the seventh century but the centuries before when there is no real evidence for this type of society in Scotland. We have seen that the situation in England was different due to the effect of having been under direct Roman rule for centuries. The expansionist policies of Northumbria in the seventh century undoubtedly influenced a growth towards more centralised polities or societal groupings in Strathclyde, Pictland and probably Dalriada. It has been suggested that Northumbria was initially formed by Germanic-speaking mercenaries and incoming settlers banding together. Dalriada had already been pushed in this direction by the activities of Columba. This would not have been the situation in the early sixth century. Bede also tells us that the organisation of the Columban church was different from that of Rome, with abbots being more powerful than bishops and having a different and more archaic way of calculating Easter. This control by abbots is significant in that in the rest of Christianity the bishops were part of a hierarchical structure that increasingly saw Rome as its apex. The Columban church appears to be much more locally based and in this it might well have paralleled the tribal structure, having a distinct territory or sharing the territory of the tribe. It is significant that Columba was himself a man of standing within his native community and that he became actively involved in the politics of Dalriada claiming that Aedan should be 'king' because of a dream sent from God. The differences between the Roman and the Columban churches, which included a distinctive tonsure among the Columbans with the front of the head shaven, suggested as originating among the Druids, were resolved at the Synod of Whitby in 664 in favour of the Roman party. However, some monks continued to follow a more independent line and, known as Culdees, continued in existence at some of the more major religious sites in Scotland until the fourteenth century.

Vanora's Stone, Meigle
Said in local tradition to show Vanora (Guinevere) about to be torn to death by wild dogs for her crimes.

Vanora's Stone (detail)
The standard interpretation has this as Daniel in the
Lion's Den from the Christian Bible. The Picts used both pagan and
Christian motifs on their symbol stones.

Dunadd
Entrance to the hill-fort of Dunadd in the Kilmartin valley,
capital of the Scottish Kingdom of Dalriada throughout the Dark Ages.

Edinburgh Castle

- one-time important site of the Gododdin tribe, long known as the Castle of Maidens, as it was in the 18th century. St Monenna site.

Stirling Castle

Dark Age fortified site, possibly of the Gododdin, overlooking the Gap of Stirling, site of many battles over hundreds of years. St Monenna site.

Vanora's Mound, Meigle Kirkyard

- Such curses were heaped over Vanora's grave that any woman standing on the mound was said to have been made immediately sterile.

Dumbarton Rock

Traditionally associated with Arthur and later the capital of the British kingdom of Strathclyde. From certain angles, the rock is clearly breast-shaped.

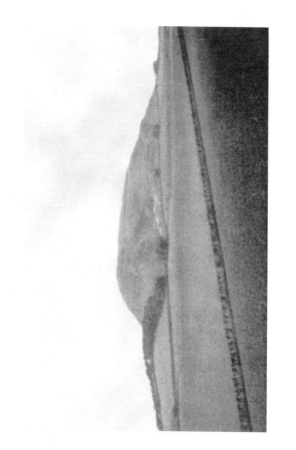

Traprain Law

Important Gododdin site where King Lot of the Lothians was said to rule and where Modred, Gawain and St Thenew originated. St Monenna site.

Castle Campbell, Dollar

Striking site which corresponds to medieval description of the Arthurian castle of the Dolorous Gard. Streams behind it called Burn of Care and Burn of Sorrow.

Corryvreckan whirlpool
The Cauldron of the Goddess between the islands of Scarba and Jura
– at certain times of the year a truly awesome site – with Scarba in the foreground.

Ben Arthur

Striking mountain at the head of Loch Long thought to have been named after the heroic tribal warrior Arthur.

Eildon Hills, Melrose

Strong traditional associations with Arthur and Thomas the Rhymer.
Earlier the site of the Roman fort of Trimontium. Melrose is an important Early Christian site.

Bennachie

Mountain in Aberdeenshire, with prominent nipple-shaped feature called Mither Tap.
At one time a large cairn called Arthourscairne was visible on the south side of the summit.

Arthur's Seat, Edinburgh
It was said Arthur and his knights lie sleeping here, waiting to be called
to come to the aid of Scotland. St Anthony's chapel in the foreground.

Tinto Hill, near Biggar
The Hill of Fire, site of ritual fire festivals of
Beltane and Halloween and suggested target of the battles on the
nearby River Douglas.

Aberlemno Kirkyard Stone
Pictish Symbol Stone showing 7th century battle scene between the
Picts and Northumbrians, showing the type of weaponry probably used by
Arthur and his warriors.

THE WELSH ANNALS

The Welsh Annals (Annales Cambriae) survive in three ancient manuscripts, the earliest being appended to the *Historia Brittonum*, attributed to Nennius and thought to date originally from the second half of the tenth century, though we only have later copies. They mention the Battle of Badon in 516 and that Arthur was victorious after he had carried the cross of Christ on his shoulders for three days and three nights. The modern interpretation of the reference to the cross is that it was an emblem on Arthur's shield, something that was commonplace in later centuries among the Crusaders. This reference stands out amongst the others, partly because it is longer than most but also in that it is particularly detailed. We are told specifically that Arthur was carrying or wearing the cross of Christ which suggests that his role in this battle had something to do with the Christian religion. Although Picts, Scots and Saxons are all referred to as pagans in many early sources, by the sixth century some of the Picts had supposedly been Christianised by St Ninian, based at Whithorn on the Solway Firth in the early years of the fifth century, and St Patrick had been actively making Christian converts among the Scots of Ireland up until his death around 457. It is therefore significant who Arthur's opponents at Badon were. Skene suggested that the Battle of Badon Hill was likely to have been fought at Bouden Hill near Linlithgow in West Lothian, with all of the 12 battles mentioned by Nennius taking place in central Scotland. This would indicate that the opponents were either Picts, Scots or other Britons. The reference to the cross in this context I suggest makes it clear that his opponents were pagan, whatever their linguistic or ethnic origin. St Patrick in his letter to Coroticus refers to the Picts turning away from Christianity after the time of Ninian. It is not impossible that he was facing a mixed force of Britons, Picts and Scots, and even Angles, the Saxons being in the south of Britain.

Alliances between them had, after all, been in existence since at least the fourth century, as the Romans found to their cost.

The only other mention of Arthur in the *Annals* is for the year 537 in which he is said to have to have fallen, along with Medraut (Modred) at the Battle of Camlaan. They also say that there was a plague in Britain at this time. We will look in detail at this location but it is worth noting that Medraut (Modred) was the son of Lot of the Lothians who in *Life of Kentigern* is clearly presented as being a pagan. As I have stated, storytelling, the primary means of oral transmission, would have its tales located within the local environment of the group or tribe in which the tale was told, making Arthur just as real for the Welsh tribes as for their cousins in north Britain, but the weight of evidence for most of the action attributed to Arthur taking place in what is now central and southern Scotland is overwhelming.

NENNIUS

Alongside the *Welsh Annals* in the manuscript *Harleian* 3859 in the British Museum is the *Historia Brittonum (The History of Britain)*, an early attempt at history attributed to Nennius and dating from the early years of the ninth century. It is very much a jumble of materials referring to earlier periods and it is generally accepted that such works would have drawn upon even earlier manuscripts of annals and other materials. It is also a possibility that at least some of the monks involved in the compilation of early manuscripts had access to local traditions that were essentially oral. The *Historia Brittonum* is now thought to have been compiled in the first half of the ninth century, 300 years after the time of the historical Arthur. The work contains lives of saints, excerpts from chronicles and, most importantly for our purposes, a section on the campaigns of Arthur. It is worth quoting the opening paragraph of this section:

> At that time the English increased their numbers and grew in Britain. On Hengest's death, his son Ochta came down from the north of Britain to the kingdom of the Kentishmen, and from him are sprung the kings of the Kentishmen. Then Arthur fought against them in those days, together with the kings of the British; but he was their leader in battle. (56 p. 29)

It seems explicit that Nennius thought of Arthur as fighting in the south of Britain. However, the list of battles that follows can all be shown to have solid locations in Scotland. In this we should remember that Nennius was writing 300 years after the fact and presumably in the south of Wales. As noted earlier we have no documentation from the same period originating in the north. It is also the case that any material that he had gathered from oral traditions would refer to locations in Wales. Although we are reliant on monks such as Nennius for what little access we have to such remnants of traditional belief we should remember that just because a story has been written down does not mean it ceases to be told. In this respect the tenacity of oral tradition may mean we should be prepared to consider whether we can learn from material written down from oral transmission much later than the period under consideration. A story that reached me recently, that Arthur threw Excalibur into Loch Moan in Galloway, might well be a surviving remnant of original local lore. The loch is overlooked by a hill called Suie Hill. Could this be a similar instance to that noted by W. J. Watson (p. 208): 'Suidhe Artair, Suiarthour 1638 . . ., now Suidhe, in Glenlivet, Banffshire'? This part of south-west Scotland was P-Celtic-speaking up until the early Middle Ages.

There are a couple of other intriguing references to Arthur worth looking at. In the section of Nennius called 'The Wonders of Britain' he mentions two places in Gwent in Wales. The first is a place called Builth where a heap of stones, or cairn, is said to have a dog's footprint on it. This, he says, was left by Arthur's hound when its master was hunting Twrch Trwyth Cafal. The cairn was said to have been raised by Arthur and 'Men come and take the stone in their hands for the space of a day and a night, and on the morrow it is found upon the same pile.' (p. 41) Here we seem to have a garbled memory of some ancient pagan rite. The hunting of Twrch Trwyth Cafal occurs in the story of Culhwch and Olwen in *The Mabinogion* as part of a series of magical tasks that Culhwch must undertake before he can marry Olwen. The tasks are set by the Giant Ysbaddaden, Olwen's father and he has to be shaved with a razor and comb that are between the ears of the magical boar Twrch Trwyth. The quest results in widespread devastation in Britain and Ireland. This tale is patently mythological and the assault on Twrch Trwyth and her piglets might signify an assault on paganism as there are many instances in both Welsh and Irish mythology where such creatures are closely linked to goddess figures. While the battles mentioned by Nennius seem to be historical this reference is clearly to pre-Christian beliefs supporting the idea of Arthur as both a mythological and historical figure. The second wonder associated with Arthur mentioned by Nennius is also suggestive of ancient belief. This is the tomb by a spring at a place called Ergyng called Llygad Amr, in which a warrior called Amr was buried. 'He was a son of the warrior Arthur, and he killed him there and buried him. Men come to measure the tomb, and it is sometimes six feet long, sometimes nine, sometimes twelve, sometimes fifteen. At whatever measure you measure it on one occasion, you never find it again of the same measure, and I have tried it myself.' (ibid) This seems very similar to the widespread folklore idea that it is impossible to be certain as to the numbers of stones in certain stone circles. What this means exactly is difficult to define, which may be the point of such stories – that the old ways are beyond modern, rational, Christian understanding but preserve a magical continuity with ancient belief. Arthur's slaying of his son here is reminiscent of Cu Chullain killing his son in Irish tales and has the aspect of a tale showing that we are all the subjects of fate. Nennius may have been a monk but here he is recording garbled versions of what are surely ancient mythological tales.

THE WELSH TRIADS

The Welsh Triads are a collection of Welsh poetry surviving in thirteenth- and fourteenth-century manuscripts believed to have been copied from earlier versions compiled in the eleventh and twelfth centuries. They are arranged in threes though some of the Arthurian references are added on to make a group of four. Grouping facts in threes is a well known procedure that helps memorising, which would have been particularly important in societies where all knowledge had to be held in the memory before it could be passed on. What seems clear is that these originated in earlier oral tradition and may reflect what were once aspects of pagan belief. Some of the same motifs turn up in sections of *The Mabinogion*. Given what we now know of oral transmission it is possible some of the content originated in the sixth century or even earlier. In the Triads Arthur is presented as King ruling over most of Britain from his court in Cornwall, though the idea of Arthur as a king probably originates in the early Middle Ages. The versions mentioned here are from the 1978 version *The Welsh Triads*, edited by R. Bromwich. It is noticeable that although Arthur is a king in the Triads the references are not all complimentary, something we see echoed in medieval Scottish sources. He is referred to as one of *The Three Frivolous Bards of Britain* (p. 21) and as one of *The Red Ravagers of Britain* (p. 35), due no doubt to the number of battles he was involved in. In *The Three Powerful Swineherds of Britain* it is said he tried to get a pig by deceit and force but was unsuccessful. Arthur's actions here might echo back to the same sort of belief that underpinned the concept of Twrch Trwyth. According to Triad 37R (p. 89), Arthur dug up the head of Bran which had been buried on London's White Hill in the Mabinogion tale of Branwen, Daughter of Llyr. The head was there to protect the island from the plague, which might refer to the idea of invasion, and Arthur thought it unseemly that any-one but himself should be the protector of the island. In the Triads when Arthur fights Modred at the Battle of Camlaan, Modred is leading an alliance of Picts, Saxons and Scots. According to the Triads Arthur had left the country to extract tribute from the Roman Empire! *Three Harmful Blows of the Island of Britain*, (p. 144) says the Battle of Camlaan was caused by Gwenhwyfach striking Gwenhwyfar (Guinevere – the closeness of these names suggest a faded memory of some ancient goddess, a motif perhaps repeated in Triad 56 where Arthur is said to have had three queens, all called Guinevere) and Triad 57 tells us he had three mistresses, hardly an ideal sort of behaviour for a Christian king. *One the Three Unfortunate Counsels of the Island of Britain* (p. 159), has an intriguing reference to the Battle of Camlaan, which is men-tioned five times in the Triads, suggesting it was seen as having been of some importance, namely 'the three-fold dividing by Arthur of his men with Medrawd [Modred] at Camlaan.' It is an intriguing possibility that this might actually be a reference to how the battle had been fought half a millennium before the Triads were written down, though Bromwich sees this as referring to Arthur having given a third of his men to Modred before setting off for Rome. In tribal terms this would make no sense – on his return surely such warriors would have refused to fight against him.

Bromwich comments that accounts of this battle were promi-nent in Arthurian stories up to the time of Geoffrey of Monmouth in the twelfth century. She also draws attention to a passage from the early Welsh tale *The Dream of Rhonabwy* in which Iddawg son of Mynio claims he got his nickname the Embroiler for hav-ing distorted the message sent by Arthur to Modred before the Battle of Camlaan. He claimed it was as a result of this the battle took place. Triad 85 (p. 211) says one of Arthur's three principal courts was at Penrhyn Rhionydd in the north. This has been interpreted as being a fort on the Rhinns of Galloway in south-west Scotland and suggests an ongoing awareness of the ease of sea travel up and down the west coast of Britain in Welsh tradition. Travel by boat from here up the river Clyde to Dumbarton, Loch Long and Loch Fyne or round the Mull of Kintyre and up to the Kilmartin valley and the rest of Dalriada would be straightforward.

THE MABINOGION

The Mabinogion is the name given to a collection of Welsh tales that were first written down in the fourteenth and fifteenth centuries but clearly are developed from earlier oral transmission. It seems likely that they had been in written form since the eleventh century and are influenced by feudal and romantic ideas of kingship and chivalry, but even with these influences their portrayal of King Arthur is not always that of an idealised king. However, he is portrayed as a king with a court of knights and ladies throughout these stories. J. Markale in his book *King of the Celts: Arthurian Legends and Celtic Tradition* (p. 60) makes a telling point about these female figures: 'The ladies of Arthurian romances are reincarnations of ancient goddesses who had power of life and death.' What we see in much of this material are ancient beliefs overlaid with later Christian ideas and the social practices of periods long after the stories themselves were first told. While it is clear that the themes of the tales and perhaps even their basic narrative format are taken from earlier oral traditions, like most literature they do not show the typical aspects of oral tales that had been developed over millennia to assist their memorisation – repetition, alliteration and so on. It also seems that in some of the individual tales there has been an attempt to incorporate what was a whole collection of stories. In the story of Peredur Longspear for instance, the hero repeatedly comes to castles where he becomes involved in one kind of battle or another. All of these episodes are similar and it seems likely that in the far past each episode might have been the focus of an individual tale. It is from the tales in *The Mabinogion* that much of what we know about Arthur originates and they have many references to individuals who seem to have originated not only among the Picts but to others who clearly derive from Gaelic-speaking areas. If, as seems likely, a considerable amount of this material originated among the P-Celtic-speaking peoples of southern and central Scotland, such inclusions are hardly surprising.

CULHWCH AND OLWEN

In this story there is an extensive list of warriors at Arthur's court and though some of them have descriptive names, for example Drwst Iron-fist and Glewlwyd Mighty-grasp, none of them have aristocratic titles. This is like the listing of individual warriors in *The Gododdin* and some of the names, Drwst being one of them, are almost identical to names we know amongst the Picts, Drust being a name that occurs in the Pictish king-list. References to groups of warriors as the sons of Nudd and Caw refer to figures who we can be sure were legendary or mythological figures. This list is an example of piling together a host of mythological and legendary figures from ancient oral tradition to form a list of warriors to illustrate the glory of Arthur's court, located in several of the *Mabinogion* tales at Caerleon-on-Usk in Wales. These include Gwynn ap Nudd, the king of Annwn, the Welsh Underworld, and Manawydan son of Lyr, known in Irish and Scottish Gaelic tradition as the sea god Manannan Mac Lir. Some commentators in the past saw the stone Clach Mannan which gave rise to the place name Clackmannan, a small town on the north of the River Forth, as being the Stone of Mannan, while others see it as referring to

Manau, the land of the Gododdin tribe. Modern scholarship tends to give single isolated meanings to such objects but we cannot be sure of how names and their associated symbolism would have been interpreted by a pre-literate audience. In pre-literate societies with the corresponding reliance on memory it is surely feasible that names could have preserved complex ideas much as symbols in such societies could have a whole series of meanings. Many of the warriors are possessed of magical qualities: Sgilti Lightfoot who ran on the tops of trees and the tips of reeds; Osla Big-knife whose knife was used to bridge rivers; Gilla Stag-shank from Ireland who could jump 300 acres; and Clust, son of Clustfeinad, who could hear an ant wakening 50 miles away. Just as Gilla is clearly linked to Gaelic Ghille, a servant or lad, so Sgilti and Osla appear to be Norse names. This is hardly to be wondered at as the Norsemen had come to Scotland, Ireland and the west of England centuries before these stories were written down.

Culhwch, a warrior at Arthur's court, is told by the giant Ysbaddaden that as part of his series of magical tasks he must get Arthur and his followers to hunt Twrch Trwyth. Arthur's consent to this seems to speak more of tribal loyalty than a structured feudal hierarchy. Within the extensive list there are clear hints that there were stories in the oral tradition about certain of the individuals and groups that were not included. As storytelling was an integral part of pre-literate society for millennia it is hardly surprising that the original scribes could not write them all down. After all, the scribes' primary functions were probably religious, and vellum parchment was an expensive resource. Here, the oral practice of locating tales within the known environment of the originally tribal audience is used to give a precise location for Arthur's court, at Caerleon-on-Usk. Culhwch's father in the tale is given as Cyleddon Wledig. A great many authors have spent a great deal of time trying to show that the use of the term Wledig or Guledig proves an adherence to Roman principles, but it might just as well be an adherence to Roman literary practice; after all, we are reliant on Christian scribes writing in Latin. What is interesting is that his father's name is very similar to Celidon, the site of one of Arthur's battles, and thus almost certainly linked to Caledonia, the ancient name for Scotland.

THE DREAM OF RHONABWY

We have come across Iddawg the Embroiler in the Welsh Triads, and it is possible both references arise from an original common source. Iddawg says (G. and T. Jones, p. 116): 'Before the Battle of Camlaan I parted from them, and I went to Y Llech Las in Prydein to do penance.' Y Llech Las translates as the Blue-grey Stone but its location is very interesting. Jean Markale, who was Professor of Celtic Studies at the Sorbonne in Paris, suggested that the term Prydein arises from Pretani which was the Welsh or P-Celtic equivalent of the Gaelic Cruithne, which was what the Irish and Scots Gaels called the Picts. By this reckoning Iddawg goes from Camlaan to the land of the Picts, an idea which is supported by Bromwich, Chadwick, McQueen et al. This strengthens the idea that Camlaan is Camelon, near Falkirk on the south side of the River Forth, as the land of the Picts lay on the north side of the river. In this tale also there is an extended list of warriors. Interestingly, at the close of the tale tribute is brought to Arthur from the Isles of Greece, an idea that surely can be seen as a result of classical learning intruding into indigenous stories or an effect of literature on oral transmission. This process can be seen in the later English and Scottish pseudo-histories claiming origin from Brutus and Scota in the distant past. Such attempts were intended to give some sort of respectability to native history and tradition in terms of Biblical and classical scholarship. History was invented to conform to the dominant ideas of the time.

GWR Y GOGLEDD

Throughout early Welsh stories and poems there are references to the Gwr Y Gogledd, the Men of the North. These are the northern ancestors of the Welsh whose struggles amongst themselves and with the Angles form the background for the earliest Welsh poems. The first of these men is thought to have been Cunedda, who left Scotland for Wales with his eight sons in the fifth century. It is possible that the tribes in Wales kept in regular touch with their cousins in Strathclyde and Manau Gododdin throughout the period of Roman rule in England. As the Romans never conquered Ireland it is likely that the Irish Sea remained relatively open for communication north and south. After the departure of the Romans such contacts might well have increased. The survival of Y *Gododdin* in Wales confirms ongoing cultural contact if not later migrations from southern and central Scotland. It is significant that in these poems there is no mention of the Romans, either as a force or as models for behaviour. If Arthur, like the earlier Aurelius Ambrosius, was attempting in some way to emulate Roman practice, surely there would be some sense of this in the earliest poems? In *The British Heroic Age* (Chadwick, p. 70) R. Bromwich describes the situation in the north in the sixth and seventh centuries: 'The poems suggest a loose confederation of small kingdoms or territories ruled by chiefs who may have been wholly independent, or may have owed a loose kind of allegiance to certain outstanding chiefs, more or less as war-bands.' This is illustrative of the misunderstandings concerning tribal culture; the structure of tribal society had already shown that they could unite when necessary. The contradiction between kingship and chieftainship is obvious, but the idea that alliances would be formed of different tribal war-bands makes absolute sense. We should remember that the earliest Welsh poems were originally created for oral transmission and they were of considerable antiquity before they were written down. Bromwich tells us also: 'The elegiac poems served the interests of the heirs, by their praise of the great deeds of the ancestors.' (Ibid.) These ancestors are, in terms of the presentation of the material, common to all members of the tribe or kin group, not just the chief and his immediate family. The poems, like the myths and legends, would be told round every tribal hearth in the long nights of winter. Bromwich stresses other aspects: the poems are concerned with individuals, they lack any idea of a state or other organised polity and they make no mention of such things as national borders, urban developments and rarely even of defensive hilltop sites. All of this serves to underline the fact that the Men of the North, based in Scotland in the sixth and seventh centuries, formed, as has been suggested, a basically tribal warrior society consisting of small family-based groups. Significantly, the enemies mentioned in the poems are individual and personal.

Chapter Five

The Battles of Arthur

A GREAT DEAL HAS been made of Nennius's list of battles as providing the only potential hard data concerning Arthur. Other early references, such as in the poems of Taliesin, seem primarily mythological, though as we shall see there are those who see the poems differently. Many people have attempted to prove the locations as being in Wales, Cornwall, England and so on, but most of these interpretations have been predicated on the assumption that Arthur was fighting off invaders, primarily from the Continent, though sometimes in conjunction with Picts and Scots from what we now know of as Scotland. As I hope I have shown, this idea of widescale invasion is unsustainable in the light of modern scholarship.

Arthur is said by Nennius (p. 35) to have led the kings of Britain in a series of 12 battles. The analysis of distant eras of the past using models that occurred later has led to the assumption that sixth-century Britain was formed of a series of petty kingdoms, but we have seen that the north of Britain in the sixth century seems to have been composed of polities that were essentially tribal rather than based on any centralized form of kingship. What we know of tribal societies in this part of the world, and it was common on other parts of the planet, suggests that inter-tribal raiding was endemic. This raiding, generally assumed to have started in the Iron Age, continued as an integral part of Scottish Highland society into the eighteenth century. However, Arthur's supposed battles seem to correspond more to the idea of a modern organised military campaign than to any pattern of inter-tribal warfare. Arthur is said to have been the war leader, which conforms to tribal battle practice, but clearly what was happening was more than just raiding, which often was almost formal in its execution. We have a model for the leadership of Arthur amongst the tribes in the Roman writer Tacitus when he tells us of Calgacus leading the confederation of Caledonian tribes at the Battle of Mons Graupius. Arthur's campaign conforms at least partially to tribal practice. However, in the case of Mons Graupius there was the need to fight a major invading force, while in another example, the Jacobite rebellion of 1745–6, many of the Highland tribes united behind a single leader for a series of complex reasons that were probably much to do with the eighteenth-century terminal breakdown of tribal society. In the latter case we see tribal mores still operating in the retreat from Derby in the common belief that many of the Highland warriors, satisfied with the level of booty, returned home to bring in their crops. Although united behind a supposedly dynastic leader in the shape of Prince Charles Edward Stuart, they were neither bound by feudalistic ties to his cause, nor were they mercenaries for hire in the modern sense.

The Battle of Mons Graupius and 'the 45', one from half a millennium before and one from over a millennium after Arthur's battles, suggest that in undertaking a military campaign, and I can see no other way of describing these 12 battles, there must been some overpowering reason for the tribes to unite. This was not to fight off the Scots, whom we now know were in the west long before 500 AD, nor was it, despite what we are told by Gildas, to fight off the Anglo-Saxon invasion, which never occurred as a single strategic event. If these battles were to unite the country, as later writers such as Geoffrey of Monmouth clearly imply, why was such an essentially political attempt led by one who is not said to have been a king? I would suggest that the move towards kingship and the associated development towards what would become nation states happens after Arthur's battles. Could it be that in Arthur's campaign we are seeing the beginning of this major development in northern British history, and was there a specific reason for these actions?

Roman Britain was by its latter years, to a considerable extent, Christianised. It was the existence of Christianity within northern England that led to the establishment of the first Christian foundation in what we now call Scotland, at Whithorn in Candida Casa. Here St Ninian is said to have spread the word of Christ, going as far as converting at least some of the southern Picts. A. P. Smyth, in *Warlords and Holy Men*, makes the interesting suggestion that Candida Casa could have been directly influenced by Mediterranean Christian traditions rather than from within the Roman area of Britain. This would have been via sea contact following the ancient Megalithic sailing routes, and in this light Adomnan's mention of a ship trading to the west of Scotland from Gaul is significant. However Whithorn developed, it did instill some level of Christianity in northern Britain in the fifth century. St Patrick, in a letter to Coroticus in the later years of that century, talks of 'apostate Picts'. This is a clear implication that some of the Picts had been converted to Christianity then reverted to paganism. The point here is that it is the Picts – and remember we are dealing with the P-Celtic-speaking people(s) neighbouring directly on the Gododdin and the Britons of Strathclyde – are being Christianised, not just the P-Celtic-speaking peoples of southern Scotland. We have seen that there are grounds for believing there was regular and substantial contact between the various tribal peoples. This illustrates that society at this time was much less rigidly separated and structured than later analyses have suggested, allowing for much more interchange between different groupings than has been realised. Intermarriage was probably happening at a dynastic or chieftainship level, and it is important to remember that the function of the leaders, called kings by later historians, was inherently part of contemporary tribal society and was not above or separate from it. If this type of practice was common, or even acceptable, it seems likely there would be considerable interchange at other levels of society between the tribes. This would account for the existence of Arthurian traditions across tribal, and perhaps even linguistic, boundaries and suggests a fluidity between different groups and areas that could apply to many areas of human and social activity.

Tribal societies at this time in Scotland mainly consisted of relatively widespread small family groups with perhaps some large-scale settlements of hilltop sites which may have owed their importance as much to a sense of their inherent sanctity as to any military significance. In this light we can see that as monasteries grew in power and importance they themselves would become the focus of changing habitation and economic patterns, patterns that were to some extent incompatible with the traditional tribal arrangements. They were also run, even in the Columban church, on much more rigid hierarchic lines than would have existed in tribal society. My suggestion is that we can perhaps understand the Arthurian campaign, noted by Nennius as a Christian campaign against paganism, as represented by other tribes. Nennius, Gildas and Geoffrey of Monmouth were all Christian clerics and as such would be more sympathetic to a Christian hero than a pagan one.

Let us look at the 12 battles and the areas in which they are suggested to have been fought in Scotland. The locations are primarily those suggested by W. F. Skene, and extensively investigated by J. S. Glennie in his work *Arthurian Localities in Scotland*. I have added in two possible alternatives to their list. As a comparison with what has been the more generally accepted provenance of Arthur's battles, I include the list of the battles as proposed by G. Phillips and M. Keatman in their book *King Arthur: The True Story* which locates all but two of the battles in England and Wales.

SUGGESTED BATTLE SITES

Nennius		Phillips/Keatman	Glennie/Skene
1	Glein	River Glen, Lincolnshire	River Glen, Ayrshire
2-5	Dubglas, Linnius	Lindsey, Lincolnshire	River Douglas, Lennox
6	Bassas	Powys	Dunipace, Falkirk
7	Cat Coit Celidon	Far North	Tweeddale
8	Fort Guinnion	North	Roman Fort on Gala
9	City of the Legions	Caerleon/Chester	Dumbarton
10	Tribruit	Severn	Carse of Stirling
11	Agned	Bremenium, Rochester	Edinburgh Castle Rock
12	Mount Badon	Little Solsbury, Bath	Bouden Hill, Linlithgow

When first considering these locations originally propounded by Skene, I began to notice a recurring pattern. Many of them seem to be relatively close to sites that can be interpreted as having some central significance in prehistoric society. Many of these sites have been interpreted as being purely military, but I hope to show evidence for considering them as having some sacral importance. In the light of what we know of oral pre-Christian society, the Christian duality of the sacred and the profane was unknown, which can mean that some places that did have a defensive structure could also have had a significant ritual or sacral function. This would conform to what we know historically from other societies including Rome itself, where the most sacred temples were within the most heavily defended parts of the city – on Capitol Hill. Even in the heavily structured and urban society of the Roman Empire they had a hilltop sacred site at the very core of their lands.

RIVER LOCATIONS

Another significant fact of the battles mentioned by Nennius is that the majority of them are said to have been fought at locations identified by rivers. Rivers cover considerable territory, so why would he give such generalised indications of location? One possibility is that access to these localities was by following river valleys. This raises the possibility that however Arthur's commands were composed, they might have been carrying boats, or even constructing them after overland travels. The landscape of northern Britain in the sixth century was much more rugged than today. While for millennia sporadic and even widespread clearance of forest had been taking place to create suitable land for livestock and some arable farming, many areas of northern Britain would still be near impassable. This would be particularly true between the more heavily populated areas. The combination of uncultivated forests and boggy ground would have made the option of travelling by water, whether by sea or by river, very attractive. Even with a combined tribal force we are probably looking at numbers in the low hundreds at most; the Romans arrived with massive armies and provoked a commensurate response but we have no evidence to suggest that battles from post-Roman times through to the Middle Ages were of any great size by later standards. Small groups could carry lightweight boats, but there is a more feasible option.

As early as Megalithic times it is thought that skin boats were used for ocean travel. Megaw and Simpson in *An Introduction to British Prehistory* (p. 78) make the point that boats up to about 30 feet (9 metres) long could have been used, and that 'a type of boat similar to the Eskimo umiak . . . also survives in north-western Europe in a distant related form in the curragh of the west coast of Ireland.' It is probable that such skin boats were commonplace in the Roman and post-Roman periods among the British tribes. It would have been a straightforward process for people with such skills to make small- to medium-sized skin boats for river transport. And if the need for battle was considered serious enough to combine the forces of several tribes then surely resources to create such boats would not be hard to come by. This could be why Nennius mentions so many rivers. Seven of the twelve battles are referred to by river locations – they were being used as highways by Arthur's forces.

THE RIVER GLEIN

The first battle mentioned by Nennius is at the River Glein. Skene, followed by Glennie, saw this as being the River Glen, near Darvel in Ayrshire. This is close to Loudon Hill, a notable outcropping of rock in a flat plain, and such notable landmarks often have ancient structures on them. W. C. Mackenzie in his *Scottish Placenames* (pp. 48f.) argued that Lomond and Loudon essentially mean the same thing – elm hill – and that both names were close to Leven, the river name also deriving from the Gaelic for elm, *leamh*. There is nothing obvious on the top of Loudon Hill but less than mile away from it there is the site of a Roman fort. The Romans were usually careful about placing their forts in strategic locations. Overlooking the River Glen itself is the place name High Carlincraig. The Carlin was a name used of witches, often used of the Queen of Witches in Scots tradition, which parallels the use of Cailleach in Gaelic. I have suggested elsewhere that both terms were originally used of goddess figures. Just over a mile to the south of High Carlincraig we have the name Templehill, a farm close to another at Foulpapple. *Papple* in Scots can mean a swelling and in this there might be some remnant of the idea of *pap*, a name given to many significant breast shapes in the Scottish landscape. This ending also occurs in Cairnpapple, a dominant landmark site of great antiquity in West Lothian. Between the junction of the River Glen and the River Irvine at Darvel, and Loudon Hill three miles to the east, we also have a Priestland, and a couple of miles to the south-east a Chambered Cairn near Ladystone Linn. Two miles north-east of Loudon Hill is the site of the Battle of Stobieside, sometimes referred to as the Battle of Loudon Hill, fought in 1679 between two warring factions of Christians, the Covenanters and the supporters of the Stuart king Charles II. Another battle took place less than mile south-east, in 1307 between Robert the Bruce and invading English forces. If Arthur were leading a crusade against paganism perhaps Loudon Hill was the focus of ritual activity at the time. As happened around the Gap of Stirling, here we have a series of battles over considerable time, pointing up the strategic importance of the area or a specific site. There will be those who see all of this as mere coincidence, but to me that is a term whose meaning seems to built of excuses. Skene tells us that Arthur was more likely to have marched 'into Scotland on the West, where he would pass through the friendly country peopled by the Cymry, than through Bernicia, already strongly populated by Angles.' The Angles at this stage were pagan and thus, by my argument, the enemy. We know some of the Picts had turned away form Christianity so it is possible that some of the Britons of Strathclyde or from among the Gododdin had done the same.

THE RIVER DUBGLAS

Nennius next tells us that Arthur fought the second, third, fourth and fifth battles on the River Dubglas. This is a clear reference to the Scottish place name Douglas – the dark stream – and the translation of Nennius puts it in the county of Lindsey. Many commentators, like Phillips and Keatman, have accepted this as Lincolnshire, while Skene and Glennie argued forcibly that the original Linnius in the Latin text is more likely to have been the Lennox, the country round about Loch Lomond. The Douglas river runs into Loch Lomond through Glen Douglas which provides a gap through the mountains from Loch Long, the Loch of the Ships. Glen Douglas is about 5 miles (8 km) long which would suggest a series of very closely fought engagements. In Loch Lomond itself there is Inchnacailloch, generally interpreted as the Island of the Nun(s), but there is no physical evidence for a nunnery here. The name Cailloch, or more properly Cailleach, itself belonged in an earlier time to the Hag of Winter, one half of a truly ancient goddess figure who is balanced by, or is the other half of, Bride, Goddess of Summer. That Loch Lomond was of some importance in the sixth century is supported by the strange story given by Nennius of there being 60 islands and 60 eagles in Loch Lomond, which he refers to as Loch Leven. With 60 rivers flowing into it and just one, the Leven, flowing out of it, the loch is presented as the first of the 'Wonders of Britain'. Whether this is a reference to sacred significance (the nearby Picts did use eagles on their Symbol Stones) or whether it is some reference to warriors is impossible to discern, but there must have been some reason for such usage. Given that we know water travel was the norm, and that according to the Welsh Triads Arthur had a fort on the Rhinns of Galloway, Loch Long would provide direct access through Glen Douglas to either Loch Lomond itself or, via the loch for a force seeking to attack from the rear, to Dumbarton, the capital of British Strathclyde.

I am not totally convinced, however, of the argument for this location and would suggest another possibility. Fifteen miles (24 km) to the south-east of Loudon Hill is Glenbuck Loch, the source of the Douglas river that runs into the Clyde a few miles from Lanark, originally Llanerch, a P-Celtic name meaning the clear space, a name that crops up in a poem attributed to Merlin in *The Black Book of Carmarthen*. The preponderance of deer in Pictish sculpture, and J. G. Mackay's article in *Folklore* (no. 51, 1934) 'The Deer Cult and the Deer-Goddess Cult of the Ancient Caledonians', might suggest some pagan meaning in the name of the loch. However, the Douglas Water runs for over 17 miles (28 km) before meeting the Clyde which might be a more likely distance over which to have fought four battles than the much shorter Glen Douglas. Three miles (5 km) downriver from Glenbuck Loch is Carnmacoup where there used to be one of those substantial mounds, sometimes referred as basses, which I have suggested might have had some ritual function. Such functions might have been similar to what we know happened at similar locations known as thing-mounds among the Norse peoples. Here they met to hammer out matters of common public interest and such locations would involve some ritual behaviour. It is possible that such locations were regularly used for both types of activity: the socio-political and sacred ritual. Just three miles further down the River Douglas there is a what is called a motte, exactly the same type of structure, at the confluence with a small stream just a mile south of the town of Douglas. Just to the north of Douglas on the north side of the river is small burn or stream with the evocative name of Bloodmyresyke, the stream of the bloody moor, which has at least a suggestion of the memory of some conflict nearby. However, when we head further north we soon approach a site of definite pagan significance. Just over 5 miles (8 km) east of the river below the village of Rigside is Tinto Hill, earlier known as Tintock Tap. Tinto was earlier Tintock, deriving originally, according to W. J. Watson, from the Gaelic *teinteach* meaning 'place of fire'. This refers to the fact that this hill was the site of the great fires of Beltane (1 May) and Samhain (1 November) which were the great focal point of the pagan year in pre-Christian Scotland. The fact that the Beltane fires in particular survived into the twentieth century and have recently been revived in some places, including Calton Hill in the centre of Edinburgh, shows the capacity of old ideas to survive through remarkable changes. Tinto is also the most notable hill for many miles around and as such would be the natural focus for such events. Further to this there is a series of low hilltop sites, earthworks, ancient settlements and early Christian sites that all point to the ancient sanctity of this area. Underlining this is the place name Pap Craig on the summit of the hill, again referring us to the recurrent theme of breast shapes in the landscape that were the focus of some kind of ritual activity and belief. Next to Pap Craig is Wallace's Seat, illustrating the ongoing practice of heroes being associated with prominent natural features.

About four miles north-north-east of Tinto Hill is Arthurshields, not far from a mansion called Shieldhill. It is at least possible that the latter name might commemorate some distant battle and perhaps the former is reminiscent of one of the protagonists in such a battle. While none of this evidence is in any way conclusive by itself, the combined effect of them all is supportive of the possibility of the Douglas river having been the site of Arthur's second to fifth battles. If Arthur was leading a Christian crusade it would make sense to attack the most prominent sites of pagan activity and possibly, as suggested by Pope Gregory to Bishop Melitus, reconsecrate them to Christian use. This could perhaps explain why there is a dedication to St John at the ancient church on the north-eastern side of Tinto Hill. St John dedications do tend to be early. In the light of my suggestion as to pagan belief it is interesting that some early twentieth-century maps refer to the earthwork on the north-east side of Tinto Hill as the Druids' Temple, perhaps reflecting some local tradition. The reference to Linnius by Nennius was seen by Skene as referring to the Lennox area, while others have suggested Lothian, and this is a problem for this interpretation. However, Nennius was never in Scotland and was reporting from hundreds of miles away. This may have had an effect on the order in which he presented these battles.

THE RIVER BASSAS

Nennius tells that the sixth battle was 'on the River Bassas'. Following Skene, Glennie locates this at Dunipace, near Falkirk on the River Forth. Skene gives his reasons (Bryce, p. 36) as being the two mounds at Dunipace which he likens to the Bass at Inverurie, on the east coast south of Aberdeen, and writes that the original term Dunipais had as its second syllable another form of the term bass itself. Dun y bassas or something similar might be the origin of the name. Such prominent and perhaps even totally artificial mounds crop up in many parts of Scotland, two particularly notable ones being the Bass at Inverurie and the massive mound on which stands the church of St Vigeans, just outside Arbroath. Given the former classical and southern bias of so much Scottish history and archaeology it is hardly surprising that so many such structures have been interpreted as being of the motte and bailey type of fortification favoured by Normans. However St Vigeans is not the only early church site located on the top of such a structure and I suggest that what we see in these types of location is a clear example of the early Christian church re-using previous pagan sites. Such hills might correspond in some way to the notice taken of prominent breast- or nipple-shaped hills in so many different parts of the country. Given the triumph of Christianity and the fact that all early written records are from Christian sources, it is hardly to be wondered at that if such hills were significant in pagan practice little was said of this. As with so much of Scotland's past, archaeological investigation is the only way to find out what these massive structures were used for, and when. Skene mentions that there had been some speculation as to the Bass Rock, near North Berwick on the Firth of Forth, being this location. It is an intriguing thought that the prominent rock jutting out of the Forth might owe its name to a similarity to the prominent hills in river valleys called basses. He suggests the battle itself took place where the River Bonny flows into the Carron. If my suggestion that these battles form an orchestrated campaign against prominent pagan sites it might be that these two mounds, or some structure on them, were the target. Just a few hundred metres to the east there is the site of a Roman camp, and a few hundred metres further on is the site of a Roman fort, probably linked to the Antonine Wall a further few hundred metres to the south. In his *Geographical Collections* (p. 331), Macfarlane tells of a local tradition of a battle at Skaithmuir between the natives and the Romans after which the two hills were erected. Close by is Camelon, the site of the final, fateful battle between Arthur and Modred. Here we are close to other notable sites associated with Arthur. Nearby, Arthur's O'on, or oven, stood till the eighteenth century. This building appears to have been a Roman temple which had become associated with Arthur in later years. An interesting story about this occurs in Bower's *Scotichronicon*. He tells us that Julius Caesar came as far north as the River Forth and had the temple erected to sleep in, the stones of which he had carried around with him! The reason this Roman temple survived by the River Carron, Bower tells us, is that Julius was called away in a hurry to deal with some troublesome Gauls and didn't have time to disassemble his building! Bower tells us that Julius got word of trouble in Gaul from ships coming into the Forth, which at least has the ring of truth. We are then told (1 p. 191) it was called Arthur's O'on because Arthur was so fond of it he often came to visit it 'by way of recreation'. J. Bellenden in his translation of Boece's *Chronicles of Scotland* states (p. 123) that it was raised by the Roman general Vespasian in honour of the Emperor Claudius. He says that Vespasian stayed for a period at nearby Camelon, a contender for the site of the Battle of Camlaan and possibly the origin of Camelot. Here we are close to the River Forth and the Gap of Stirling is just a few miles upriver, through which armies heading north further into Scotland have always had to pass.

CAT COIT CELIDON

Nennius tells us that the seventh battle was in the Celyddon Forest. This battle of Cat Coit Celidon is accepted by virtually all who have looked at the Arthurian material to have happened somewhere in the Scottish Southern Uplands. The Caledonian Wood could, by what we know of the term Caledonian, have covered a great deal of the country. The two most commonly accepted place names referring to Caledonians are Dunkeld and the mountain of Schiehallion, both over 50 miles north of the Southern Uplands. Skene and Glennie placed this battle in upper Tweeddale. Skene saw the term Coit Celidon as meaning the same as Nemus Caledonis in Geoffrey of Monmouth's *Vita Merlini*, where Merlin fled after the Battle of Arderydd (Arthuret). Merlin then met St Kentigern and soon after was slain by some shepherds on the banks of the River Tweed. Local tradition locates his burial at Drumelzier, about 10 miles (16 km) from Tinto Hill. Geoffrey of Monmouth wrote *Dunmeller*. Leo Tolstoy in *The Quest for Merlin* was certain that this is the correct area. As Skene pointed out, this area was heavily forested in the past and parts of it are still referred to as the Ettrick and Selkirk forests. Referring to Nemus Caledonis, Skene is using material relevant to the Battle of Arderydd which according to various annals was fought in 573, while Arthur is supposed to have fallen at Camlaan in 537. As we shall see, there are those who consider the later date to be closer to the real date of the historical Arthur's death. Veitch suggests in *History and Poetry of the Scottish Border* that the site of the battle was 5 miles (8 km) east at Cademuir Hill near Peebles. He saw the name of the hill as deriving from an earlier form, Cad More, meaning the big battle. This notion led him to suggest that the ancient Welsh poem *Cad Godeu*, the 'Battle of the Trees', attributed to Taliesin, was a reference to this battle. The apparent mystical and magical content of this poem has given rise to much speculation,

Robert Graves' interpretation in *The White Goddess* (pp. 30f.) being that it was primarily to do with the alphabet. He saw it as being an arcane formula concerned with the ancient Pictish, and Irish, systems of ogham, or stroke writing, with the letters all corresponding to specific trees.

Ogham

Early references to ogham link it to the alphabet known as the Beth Luis Nion, meaning Birch Rowan Ash, and we do know there was a great deal of tree lore in British pagan tradition. Ogham is a system of representing letters with between one and four strokes drawn at different angles onto, or across, a stem line or in some cases the edge of a stone. The strokes are thought to basically represent fingers. It is found, primarily in Christian contexts, in both Ireland and the Pictish areas of Scotland. The Irish material is generally accepted as being relatively transparent and entirely Christian. The Pictish oghams, which occur on Symbol Stones over a considerable area, are not so clear and debate continues not only about their meaning but also what language they are written in. Some of them clearly contain names but they seem to contain elements of both Q-Celtic and P-Celtic, further fuelling the debate as to whether Pictish was in fact a truly distinct language. Suggestions have been made that the Picts spoke both P- and Q-Celtic languages. Some scholars suggest that they might even be in an early form of a Germanic language.

While this is interesting it might be significant. One of the most significant changes introduced by Christianity into Scotland, as elsewhere, was that of writing, in Latin. We have already looked at the replacement of oral transmission with written documentation of society's history and development, and the idea of the fighting alphabets as representing the viewpoints of paganism and Christianity is at the least a stimulating one. Such an interpretation might also be of considerable significance when looked at along with Hugh McArthur's startling interpretation of the Taliesin poem *Priddeu Annwn*, as a similar description of an actual battle, as we shall see. Near Drumelzier and on Cademuir Hill are hilltop structures referred to on the Ordnance Survey maps as forts, though military usage does not preclude some sacred functioning at such sites.

W. J. Watson in *Celtic Place Names in Scotland* (p. 343) tells us that Taliesin referred to a district in the north called Goddeu, a term meaning trees or a forest. He tells us Taliesin mentioned Goddeu and Rheged together, leading him to suggest that Goddeu was north and east of the district of Rheged which he placed around Carlisle and the northern banks of the Solway Firth. He suggests that this was in fact the area later known as the Forest of Selkirk in the Scottish Borders and quotes a suggestion that Manaw, which is the same as Manau Gododdin, was in fact 'in Godeu'. Depending on circumstances, alliances, disputes and so on, and remembering that there are no borders or boundaries mentioned in the early poetry, it is likely that the boundaries between sixth-century tribal areas in Scotland were more fluid than the modern concept of rigidly delineated borders between states. Apart from underlining the Scottish provenance of much ancient poetry and story surviving in Welsh, this raises the possibility that the Cad Godeu is not so mystical as it might at first seem and in fact could contain references to an actual battle, somewhere in the Borders region of Scotland, near to Cat Coit Celidon.

IN CASTELLO GUINNION

The eighth of Arthur's battles was said by Nennius to be 'in Castello Guinnion' and this has been interpreted by Skene, Glennie and others as Stow in Wedale, some 40 kilometres southeast of Edinburgh. Nennius makes the point (p. 35) that in this battle Arthur 'carried the image of the holy Mary, the everlasting Virgin, on his [shield] and the heathen were put to flight on that day.' This is quite specific as to the distinction between the Christian and the pagan forces. Skene located this battle at Stow because one of the surviving manuscript copies of Nennius's work mentions that Arthur took a piece of a cross from Jerusalem into battle here, and that fragments of this cross were preserved in a church at Wedale. This is the name given to the area around the rivers Gala and Heriot, contained in the modern parish of Stow, about 15 miles (24 km) from Peebles heading north-east, towards Edinburgh and the Forth. Skene refers to a Roman fort nearby, which he tells us accounts for the phrase 'in castello'. Glennie (p. 61) mentions a poem from *The Book of Taliesin* which refers to the White Stone of Galystem, and there was a notable stone, said to have been impressed with the foot of the Virgin, a little above St Mary's church at Stow. Glennie saw Galystem as containing Gala. The name Wedale has been interpreted as a variant on Woe-dale or Dale of Woe, so named because of the slaughter of Saxons here. W. C. Mackenzie in *Scottish Placenames* (p. 246) suggests that the name might derive from Old Norse *vé*, meaning a holy, presumably pagan place. He also tells us (ibid) that Stow has the same meaning, so perhaps we have here another instance of an earlier pagan site being re-used by the early Christian church. This is also about 6 miles (9 km) from Melrose, the site of a notable abbey and monastery in the past and mentioned by Nennius. Melrose sits in the shadow of the Eildon Hills, where the Romans had a fort they called Trimontium after the three peaks of the Eildons, within which, according to local tradition, Arthur and his knights lie sleeping, awaiting the call to come to the assistance of Scotland. The magical, or perhaps pagan religious, aura of these hills continued into the Middle Ages through the association with the prophet Thomas the Rhymer from nearby Earlston, who met the Queen of Faerie on the Eildon Hills before being taken to the

Land of Faerie for seven years. One local tradition has it that Thomas the Rhymer is involved in guiding adventurous humans to see the sleeping warriors of the Eildon Hills and this, along with his association with the Queen of the Faerie suggests some sort of continuity of ideas from pagan times. In *Scotichronicon*, Bower's fifteenth-century history of Scotland, he tells us of Arthur: 'It is commonly believed that he is still alive, and, as is sung in interludes: He is going to come again to restore the scattered and fugitive Britons to their rights.' (2 p. 59) This suggests that such traditions regarding Arthur were still extant in fifteenth-century Scotland, underlining the tenacity of orally transmitted ideas even in literate societies. Another suggestion has been made for 'in Castello Guinnion' by Hugh McArthur. This, he believes, is a reference to the battle he sees as being described in Taliesin's poem *Priddeu Annwn*. He locates this on the island of Scarba in the Inner Hebrides, overlooking the whirlpool of the Corryvreckan.

THE CITY OF THE LEGIONS

Nennius's quote 'The ninth battle was fought in the City of the Legions' has seen many commentators place this at Chester, while others have suggested the possibility of Carlisle. Securing a location for this battle in Scotland is somewhat problematic given that the Romans were never fully in occupation in Scotland and seem to have been in Scotland in periods of no more than 20 or 30 years at a time. This was sufficient time, however, for them to raise some notable buildings, on the shores of the Forth at Cramond and Inveresk and in the structure long known as Arthur's O'on near Falkirk, as well as the Antonine Wall itself. Many, though not all, of the Roman remains that still dot the Scottish landscape up the east coast and as far into the Highlands as Dull in Perthshire, though still clearly visible were usually created overnight as marching camps for the legions. Few of their structures in

Scotland were stone-built, and as such most of them can in no way be seen as a basis for long-term occupation. So where could such a place as the City of the Legions be in Scotland? Given the effort put into building the Antonine Wall and its specific geographic location at the strategic waist of Scotland, somewhere on or close to the wall itself would seem most likely. We know that Agricola supplied his legions by sea and it is therefore likely that such a place would have open access to the sea. Skene notes that in one manuscript Nennius writes 'which the British call Kaerlium'. Nennius refers to the first wonder of Britain as Loch Lomond, from which the River Leven flows down to the Clyde at Dumbarton. In the original Latin Nennius calls this the Leum. Dumbarton makes strategic sense. It commands the River Clyde and like so many other sites of Arthur's battles it has strong pagan associations. These are proved by the mention of a foundation by St Monenna here, a reference that suggests the presence of a group of pagan priestesses. There is also the much quoted 1367 charter of David II which refers to Dumbarton as 'Castrum Arthuri'. Skene also informs us that in the *Bruts*, the Welsh chronicles of the thirteenth century, there is a reference to Arthur fighting a battle at Alclyd, the ancient P-Celtic name for Dumbarton Rock. None of this is absolutely definitive but again the evidence does mount up to support this idea. Approaching from the east along the south bank of the river the rock appears to split in two and has distinct resemblance to a pair of breasts, though not particularly symmetrical ones! And, as we have seen, breast-shaped hills and mountains do seem to have had some significance in the pagan world of northern Britain. And there is no doubt that Dumbarton, as the capital of Strathclyde, was of major significance before and during the early Christian period.

Another potential site for the City of the Legions is at Camelon on the eastern end of the Antonine Wall. This is closer to many of the other battle sites and there are many Roman remains in the immediate vicinity, though much of the area has now been built over. Bellenden clearly stated that the Romans were at Camelon and this area would be one which the Roman navy would find very accessible. While Dumbarton was certainly an important site both before and after the sixth century, we have no obvious site of similar strategic importance at Camelon. However, this is close to the Basses at Dunipaice and it is noticeable that this is the only one of the battles that is referred to as having been fought at a city. Could this mean there had been a substanital urban development here and that this is what gave it its name? Its proximity to both the Antonine Wall, with the consequent lines of communication, and to the Gap of Stirling make it a tantalising possibilty.

THE RIVER TRYWFRWYD

The tenth battle was fought 'on the bank of the river Tryfrwyd' in John Morris's translation, though Skene preferred 'Treuruit'. He mentions there is some variation in the manuscripts on this point, one reading 'Trath truiriot' which he compares to poetic forms in *The Black Book of Carmarthen*, namely 'Trywruid' and 'Tratheu Trywruid'. The 'Trath' or 'Tratheu' means shore or shores. There is no river called Trywruid in Scotland, but Skene tells us (pp. 39f.) that a description of Scotland from 1165 says the British called the Forth 'Wreid'. He therefore interprets the location as meaning the Links of the Forth, the area below Stirling. As we have seen this has always been an important strategic area and thus the site of many battles over hundreds of years, and again we have the connection of Stirling Castle with St Monenna. The rock on which Stirling Castle stands is yet again a dramatic outcropping on a flat plain. It is in fact the central one of three major outcroppings here. Skene also mentions an often-quoted excerpt from William of Worcester's fifteenth-century *Itinerarium* in which he mentions Arthur as having had his round table at Stirling, or Snowdon

West. The idea of the Round Table first arises in the work of the twelfth-century French poet Wace, but as we do not know what his source for this was, or even if he invented it, this is not necessarily helpful in locating the battles. There is, however, a strange earthwork known as the King's Knot lying in the shadow of Stirling Castle which some have identified as the Round Table. Stirling is obviously a very important site but it is unclear as to who controlled it in the sixth century. Although the river may have been a natural boundary between peoples at some time there is evidence to suggest that in our period the same people lived on both sides of it immediately below Stirling. This part of Scotland was regularly the scene of battle and warfare and as such might be seen as an area where different peoples, tribes or nations would intermingle. The north side of the Forth has been interpreted as part of the Pictish province of Fortriu, with the area around Alloa and Dollar perhaps part of the province of Fib (Fife), but we also have references to a specific people or tribe in this part of the country, the Maetae, or Miathi. They are mentioned significantly by Adomnan in his *Life of St Columba* as being involved in a battle, one we will consider later. Dumyat, a hill fort overlooking Stirling in the Ochil Hills north of the river, is believed to have been one of their strongholds. However, it is at least worth considering whether Manau Gododdin came this far. It is only 7 miles (11 km) to Clackmannan, though on the north side of the Forth, the name of which, as we have seen, may refer to Manau rather than Manannan, the Q-Celtic sea god. Similarly, Slamannan on the south side of the Forth 6 miles (9 km) beyond modern Falkirk might have something of the same sense. We shall look at this area in greater detail later.

MYNYD AGNED

Nennius tells us that the eleventh battle was on the hill called Agned. Skene has no doubt that this was Edinburgh and accepted the name Mynyd Agned as referring to the location on Edinburgh Castle Rock. He makes a telling point (p. 42) when he writes: 'This battle seems not to have been fought against the Saxons.' The enemy here was said to have been the Cathregonnum or Cathbregyon, whom he sees as being Picts. Skene later (p. 111) mentions a poem from *The Book of Taliesin* which refers to the 'Catbreith of a strange language' and mentions a ford on the Carron river at Torrador. Scholarship today tends to consider the Picts as inhabiting the lands north of the Forth–Clyde line, but south of Edinburgh are the Pentland Hills and Pentland in the north is accepted as referring to the Picts. We also have the situation where Roman sources tell of 'Caledonians and other Picts' early in the fourth century AD, and the fact that the Caledonian Forest at least stretched considerably further south. We do not know how these people described themselves but from what we know of tribal societies, in Scotland and Ireland as well as elsewhere, it seems clear that alliances between different groups had the capacity to change rapidly and were more fluid than relationships between later nation states and kingdoms. I see the reference to St Monenna foundations as suggesting earlier pagan practices on sites probably re-used by the Christians. Given its location and defensive capabilities it was probably of great importance long before the Romans arrived. Although we have no record of Roman occupation on the rock of Edinburgh Castle itself, there is substantial evidence for them having occupied areas at Inveresk and Cramond, both on the outskirts of the modern city of Edinburgh. Yet again we have a location with a dramatic hilltop site, suggestions of pagan activity and nearby Roman activity. Bower in his *Scotichronicon* (1 p. 235) says the city was called

Agned by the Britons but that it was 'restored by Aed, King of the Scots', probably meaning Aedan Mac Gabhran. This, he says, is what gave rise to the modern name Edinburgh, from Aedanburgh. If this was based on an actual tradition of Bower's time it underlines the intermingling and fluidity of relationships between the different peoples and tribes of Scotland in the sixth century. We have also seen that this is a prime candidate for the location of the original Castle of Maidens in Arthurian romance.

MONS BADONICUS

The twelfth battle mentioned by Nennius is Badon Hill, or 'Mons Badonicus'. This name has led many commentators to suggest it was somewhere near Bath. However, it is relatively certain that Nennius was writing his work in north Somerset and this would surely have led him to make some comment if this fateful final battle was fought so close by. This is the battle also mentioned by Gildas and is thought to have been fought in 516 AD. Skene (p. 44) refers to the fact that Arthur's opponent here was the Saxon Ossa Cyllelaur, whom he considers to be the Octa mentioned by Nennius. We know that alliances between Picts, Scots and Saxons had been happening since the fourth century at least, so finding Saxons in Scotland in the sixth century should not be considered remarkable. Such an alliance could well have been re-forged in reaction to a Christian crusade by British warriors under the leadership of Arthur. It is within the bounds of possibility that these various pagan peoples coming together through established practice triggered Arthur's campaign. Historians have continually underestimated the importance of water travel and when we consider that it is quicker to sail from the east of Scotland to the Low Countries than to the south of England in certain wind conditions, then communication between Picts or Scots and the Germanic-speaking tribes of north-western Europe would not have been difficult, or even unusual. Skene located this battle on Bouden Hill, near Linlithgow, 15 miles (24 km) from Edinburgh and close to the southern bank of the River Forth. Mentioning that 'the scene of the battle near Bath was said to be on the Avon' (p. 44) he points out that Bouden Hill overlooks a river Avon, a name common to both P- and Q-Celtic. Further to this there are the remains of defensive hilltop structures here and on the nearby hill of Cockleroy. Glennie, investigating this location, was told by an old man he met near Bouden Hill in 1869 that there was a 'Fechtin Fuird', or fighting ford, below Bouden Hill and that the nearby Cockleroy Hill got its name 'because the king was cockled [cuckolded] there'. The old man went on to say that he hadn't heard who the king was but that, 'It's mentioned in history that King Arthur's wife was not faithful, and maybe it was her that was overly intimate with another ane on the top there.' (p. 47) Given what we now know of the tenacity of oral tradition, this can be seen as giving some support to the idea that this was the site of one of Arthur's battles. The same informant told Glennie that more than a thousand years before in the area 'there were just various wild tribes all fighting among each other' (ibid). In the light of my suggestion as to the battle being perhaps associated with places of significant pagan importance, less than 2 miles (3 km) to the south of Bouden Hill is Cairnpapple, yet another striking outcrop of rock in the landscape which was of ritual significance as far back as Megalithic times. We are close here to both Edinburgh and Falkirk, round which we have located a number of these battles. What is particularly significant about this battle is that it is also mentioned in the *Annales Cambriae* for the year 516, though modern interpretations would suggest 518.

M. Stephens in his 1998 *New Companion to the Literature of Wales* (p. 22) suggests that as some of the battles mentioned by Nennius rhyme with each other, for example Dubglas/Bassas, Celidon/Guinnion/Badon, they derived initially from an early

Welsh poem 'so that their value as historical evidence is dubious'. It is possible to argue the exact opposite. Because the information survived in poetic form it would be easier to remember for those involved in passing on knowledge and tradition within a pre-literate society. Although by the sixth century we have expanding Christian activity and a corresponding increase in literacy, this would apply only to those working within the church and the majority of the population, living in tribal groups, would continue to function in an effectively non-literate society. This can be interpreted as suggesting that the battles of Nennius were in fact well grounded in tradition and thus worthy of our consideration. Events don't occur because they are written down; writing down what happened is one way of remembering in a social context, oral transmission another.

If Stephens' contention is correct and the memory of the battles survived until Nennius's time through oral transmission in a poem, perhaps what we are seeing is a tale, not of 12 separate battles but of a concerted campaign. The remarkable occurrence of Roman sites near these battles suggests that these locations had been important centuries before Arthurian times and had held on to this significance. My suggestion that they were all notable centres of pagan activity or power would not be diminished by this. The idea that there was a concerted attempt at a series of pre-selected pagan targets, however, is somewhat weakened by the order of the battles themselves. If they were fought in the order given by Nennius, though he does not explicitly say so, then a concerted campaign would have involved considerable criss-crossing of central and southern Scotland. There are other possibilities. As we have already noted, the importance of 'historical' material within oral societies is not bound by the same insistence on chronological and even geographical exactitude that literate history demands. If the material was handed down in a form of recitative verse then can we conceive that the order of the battles could be altered to better fit a rhyme scheme? My reasons for even considering this are that when looking at a map of central Scotland there are two routes that a concerted campaign might theoretically have followed that can be read in to Nennius's list. They are differentiated by the location of the two Douglas rivers.

The Campaign Trail

Following Skene's suggestions the force would have gone 50 miles (80 km) from the River Glen in Ayrshire to Glen Douglas by Loch Lomond, then more than 30 miles (48 km) to Dunipace, after which they would have travelled over 40 miles (64 km) to the Tweeddale area. From here to Stow is around 23 miles (37 km) and on to Edinburgh another 22 miles (35 km). If we accept Skene's contention that Dumbarton was Nennius's city of the Legions they then travelled back across Scotland for a distance of around 80 miles (128 km). They then would go to Stirling some 32 miles (50 km) back to the east and then another 35 miles (56 km) to Edinburgh, after which they would double back 15 miles (24 km) to the final battle at Bouden Hill. These distances are approximate and make no allowance for the type of terrain covered, though I assume wherever possible river travel would be preferred. However, these are considerable distances to be travelled even by lightly armed and experienced warriors. The logistical problems of such travels increase with distance and we can be sure that Arthur was leading a combined force of several war bands with the attendant problems of feeding and supplying them.

Accepting Skene's suggestion of the Glen Douglas battles taking place in the Lennox it seems clear that the Arthurian troops would be heading east towards Loch Lomond rather than away from it into the mountains. This would make sense if they were making a flanking attack on Dumbarton Rock which Skene says is the site of the ninth battle. From here, the site of Nennius's tenth battle is about 32 miles (51 km) away, though Dunipace, site of the sixth battle, is a mere 6 miles (10 km) away. However, there is a fair distance between Tweeddale and Stow. Looking at the map another possibility suggests itself, particularly if the attacks were on sites of pagan importance. This would entail the force arriving at the River Glen, possibly from Arthur's fort on the Rhinns of Galloway, then heading to the Douglas Water near Carnamcoup and on to nearby Tinto Hill. From there the route would be to Cat Coit Celidon, somewhere near Drumelzier, and on to Stow, following which they would attack Edinburgh, go on to fight the Battle of Badon at Linlithgow then on to Dunipace and the Links of the Forth near Stirling. All the distances in this scenario are considerably shorter, the longest being around 23 miles (37 km). This route would also avoid doubling back and forth across the country. This leaves out Dumbarton which Skene saw as the City of the Legions. I have suggested that perhaps the City of the Legions was at Camelon, or close to the eastern end of the Antonine Wall. In the early part of the seventeenth century George Buchanan in *Rerum Scoticorum Historia* tells of the remains of an urban settlement exactly where the Antonine Wall met the Carron River. The eighteenth-century English antiquarian William Stukely also mentioned the outlines of streets and the foundations of buildings in this area, in his account of Arthur's O'on. This, suggested by several people as the original Camelon, would seem to be a candidate for the City of the Legions and is very close to the sites of many other battles. It was perhaps so called to differentiate it from the later Battle of Camlaan which figures so strongly in Welsh tradition.

THE BATTLE OF CAMLAAN

In the *Annales Cambriae*, surviving in a tenth-century manuscript, there is the following for the year 537 or 539: 'The strife of Camlaan in which Arthur and Modred perished. And there was a plague in Britain.' As Professor Lesley Alcock pointed out in *Arthur's Britain* (p. 48), all of the other personages in these annals are known to have been real people, so it seems sensible to accept Arthur and Modred also as historical personages. As I have argued, this does not preclude the possibility of an earlier, mythological Arthur but it is one of the strongest reasons for believing there was a real person of that name in sixth-century north Britain. The tradition that Camlaan was Camelon, near Falkirk, given the probability of the other Arthurian battles happening close by, seems unassailable. As I have suggested, this could be the site of the battle Nennius refers to at the City of the Legions, and this is one of the few parts of Scotland where extensive and obvious Roman ruins were visible for centuries after they left. The reasons for this battle that have come down to us have been affected by the later romance tradition, telling us that Arthur, having conquered Britain, went off on a pilgrimage to Rome and in his absence Modred took over the throne and started ruling with Guinevere as his queen. This is nonsensical in that Arthur was never ruler of all Britain or, from what we know, a king, but it is clearly stated that Modred and Arthur fought. Modred is said by Geoffrey of Monmouth, writing over half a millennium later, to have been the son of King Lot, a king of the Picts and to whom Arthur gave that part of Scotland known as the Lothians. There is no king in the Pictish king-list that corresponds to this, but significantly Lot is referred to as pagan in Joceline's *Life of Kentigern*. Could Modred have been trying to revive the pagan religion after a successful Arthurian campaign to impose Christianity and this was the real reason for the Battle of Camlaan?

There is no doubt that this battle was seen as significant amongst the British peoples as it crops up several times in Welsh tradition. It is referred to several times in the tale of *Culhwch and Olwen* and in *The Dream of Rhonabway*; in the latter case the warrior Iddawg the Embroiler claims that he caused the battle by distorting the message he carried from Arthur to Modred. In the Welsh Triads the battle is said to have occurred after Arthur went to the Continent to demand tribute from the Roman emperor, an idea that probably came from Geoffrey of Monmouth's fantastic *History of the Kings of Britain*, but it also says Arthur was taken off, to be buried in the Island of Affalach, which is clearly Avalon. Geoffrey of Monmouth gives greater detail of this in his *Life of Merlin* where he says that Arthur was taken off to the Isle of Avalon by Morgan and her sisters (in *The Quest for the Nine Maidens* I show that these are clearly pagan priestesses, which is problematic as Arthur was clearly Christian). It is thought that Geoffrey of Monmouth had access to earlier texts and extant traditions and I would suggest that the Triads and Geoffrey's accounts can be understood if we accept that we are dealing with material that contained references to pagan beliefs. Geoffrey was writing a good story rather than anything approaching an attempt at what we nowadays call history and incorporated a wide range of material. Geoffrey was aware of the tradition of the nine priestesses of Avalon and might easily have added some colour to the suggestion that Arthur was buried on this island. If Camlaan was an actual battle and the fallen victorious leader was taken off to be buried we have a model in Scottish historical practice in the Isle of Iona. Arthur was not a king but his role as a significant leader would surely have afforded him honour in death. As we have seen, traditional tales in pre-literate societies are generally presented within the known environment of the audience. In this case there is a good location for Avalon within the environs of the Forth, the river close to Camlaan/Camelon. This is the Isle of May out in the Firth of Forth, an island whose name means precisely the Isle of the Maiden(s). Recent excavations have proved that this was a sacred site in both pre-Christian and early Christian times. Was Arthur taken off to be buried on the Isle of May, and Geoffrey took this tradition and gave us the transporting of the wounded king to the mystical Isle of Avalon where he lived on? Remembering that this took place in the sixth century and that perhaps burial on the island was seen as a mark of respect in its own right, we should not be surprised if there was no great monument to Arthur. Could it even have been that his remains were among the skeletons found in early Christian burials in the 1990s?

There is another practice that might hark back to the distant past that can be seen in the story of the fateful Battle of Camlaan. Recent research has shown that the often derided idea of matrilineal descent amongst the Picts might have in fact existed. This would mean that the right of sovereignty would descend through a female line and a king would attain his position through marrying the queen. It has been noted on many occasions that there are several names in the Pictish king-list that appear to be from other areas or polities in Scotland. Here the idea would be to bring in a powerful man from another tribe or nation who was fit to marry the queen. If this was the case in the marriage of Modred to Guinevere, are we seeing the queen attempting to return to traditional pagan ways, after rejecting the Christian Arthur? There are a number of Pictish Symbol Stones which are clearly pagan on one side and Christian on the other side which reinforces the idea that there was a period when the two religions were in existence simultaneously, so an ongoing period of struggle between them would be possible. Nennius's statement that he led the kings into battle might refer to an attempt to re-impose Christianity by a combined force after such a reversion to paganism.

Whatever actually happened it seems that Camlaan kept a strong hold on the public imagination for a considerable time and became a standard motif in the traditions that have survived in Welsh literature. We have looked at Arthur's battles in Scotland which, apart from the possibilities of Glen Douglas being at Loch Lomond and the City of the Legions being Dumbarton, are all fought in the centre and the east. In the west, Dalriada was probably

Christian before Columba's arrival there in 563. There are grounds for thinking some of south-west Scotland had likewise been Christianised from the time of St Ninian a century earlier. Against this there is the suggestion that Arthur did in fact fight on the west, specifically attacking a temple site on the isle of Scarba.

Chapter Six

Geoffrey of Monmouth

THE IMPACT GEOFFREY OF MONMOUTH'S *The History of the Kings of Britain* had in spreading the popularity of Arthur and The Matter of Britain, as it has been called, was considerable. If we look at what Geoffrey tells us of Arthur we can perhaps discern some of the original ideas about Arthur behind his portrait of the idealised feudal king. Geoffrey described himself as a modest Briton but his original name, Gaufridus Monemutensis, is a Latinised Norman name so perhaps he was a descendant of one of the Bretons who had come over with William the Conqueror in 1066. This would account for the sympathy he seems to show towards Brittany and Cornwall, both P-Celtic-speaking areas in the sixth century and separated by the English Channel. Communication between these areas since prehistoric times has ensured a cultural continuity of language, myth and legend. Today the Breton language still flourishes, while in Cornwall the old P-Celtic language is spoken by some people who have revived the language from literary sources. Geoffrey was a priest, working as a teacher in Oxford when he wrote *The History of the Kings of Britain* between 1136 and 1138. His audience was among the aristocratic Anglo-Normans who ruled England at the time and his version of events reflects this. However, his sympathy for the Bretons and Cornish seems to have certainly led him to include material that derived ultimately from the oral traditions of these peoples. There is little doubt that Cornwall, and thus Brittany, was heavily influenced by tradition and belief in Wales and as we have seen much traditional Welsh material was once commonplace in what we now know as Scotland. Geoffrey said that he had been given the book 'in the British language' by Walter, the Archdeacon of Oxford, which he said he did little more than translate into Latin. However the long and often fantastic story which Geoffrey tells seems to owe a great deal to his imagination – he was telling a story intended to show the ongoing magnificence of the English monarchy. The claims to be dealing with Britain as a whole are ironic in view of the ensuing struggles between England and Scotland over the next 500 years. In fact, works such as Geoffrey's were sometimes used to try and justify attempted English conquests of Scotland. As R. S. Loomis wrote in his article *Scotland and The Arthurian Legend* (p. 7):

> When Edward I in 1301 had his secretaries draw up a statement of his rights to the overlordship of Scotland, they based it largely on Geoffrey's *Historia*. It is not unlikely that the Oxford magister, sitting at his desk, had a fatal influence on Scottish–English relations, and it was all done by scribbling a few lines with his quill pen.

It possible that the book in the British language referred to by Geoffrey was a copy of Nennius as there are passages in Geoffrey's work that are clearly taken from Nennius – though usually expanded in Geoffrey's imagination. It is from this work that the romantic idea of King Arthur, his Knights of the Round Table and all the chivalric magnificence of an idealised feudal court ultimately derive. He knew his audience. His later work *The Life of Merlin* shows that he had access to traditional tales among the P-Celtic-speaking tribes deriving from pre-Christian times before literacy arrived. So, despite his florid imagination and the obvious propagandist intent of the *History*, we can perhaps see remnants of what were contemporary traditions referring back to the sixth century.

Geoffrey presents us with an idealised portrait of a fifteen-year-old King Arthur 'of outstanding courage and generosity, and his inborn goodness gave him such grace that he was loved by almost all the people.' This sets the tone of the rest of his story of

Arthur. He says his first battle was beside the River Douglas and was against a combined force of Saxons, Scots and Picts. This is the same make-up of forces as the in fourth-century Roman sources and it is possible that Geoffrey had access to Roman texts as well as Nennius. It also stresses the fact that we have strong evidence for alliances between these different peoples over considerable periods of time, though there is no reason to see such behaviour as in any way akin to a formal alliance between states or kingdoms. Such alliances are much more likely to have been temporary arrangements primarily concerned with raiding for gain. After all, as we have seen, inter-tribal raiding was standard practice among the Celtic-speaking peoples and is just as likely to have been the norm amongst the Germanic-speaking tribes. The modern conception of the movement of Germanic-speaking peoples into Britain happening over an extended period suggests different tribal groups arriving piecemeal rather than any centrally organised campaign. Geoffrey later describes Arthur pursuing the Saxons (no mention here of Scots or Picts) to Celidon Wood. This again matches with one of the battles of Nennius, the Battle of Celidon Wood.

He gives a rather precise description of what happened here. The Saxons were hiding in the wood and Arthur ordered the trees surrounding the area they were in to be cut down and erected to form a stockade. His idea was to starve them out, and after three days without food the Saxons made a bargain with him that if they left all their gold and silver – booty from raiding – they would be allowed to return to their boats and sail back to Germany. They added that they would send tribute to Arthur and leave hostages with him. However, being the 'bad guys' in this story once they had set sail they changed their minds and returned to Britain, landing at Totnes and ravaging the countryside as far as the Severn. It is a pretty fair distance from the Scottish Borders to Totnes in the far south-west of England. Geoffrey goes on (p. 217) to relate that Arthur then took his men down to Bath where he again defeated the Saxons. He describes him going into battle with:

> Across his shoulders a circular shield called Pridwen, on which there was painted a likeness of the Blessed Mary, Mother of God, which forced him to be thinking perpetually of her. He girded on his peerless sword Caliburn, which was forged in Avalon. A spear called Ron graced his right hand; long broad in the blade and thirsty for slaughter.

The reference to the shield is a clear echo of Nennius, but in telling us the sword Caliburn was forged in Avalon we are perhaps seeing something that had originated in pagan times; after all, Avalon was hardly a Christian idea. This section reads more like a pagan warrior praise poem than a panegyric to a Christian knight. It is intriguing that the shield is called Pridwen, which seems to be the same as Prydein or Prydyn, a term generally thought to refer to the lands of the Picts. Throughout his tale of Arthur, Geoffrey is at pains to point out that he is fighting pagans, and in some of the text there is a rampant bloodthirstiness that reminds us that in many instances the imposition of Christianity itself was a brutal business. This is something on which more recent historians of the church have understandably not wanted to focus. Better, as in Scotland, to present a Christian hero like Columba as a truly saintly figure of great virtue and ability, this despite the fact that Columba had Christian blood on his hands.

After defeating the Saxons at Bath, Arthur then rushes back up to Alcluyd (Dumbarton) where the Picts and Scots were besieging his nephew Hoel. This again might originate in Nennius and there is also the reference to a battle here in the *Bruts*. Then Arthur sets off for Moray, on the Pentland Firth in the north of Scotland, where he fought with the Picts and Scots again. Moray was always one of the power centres of the Picts and for a long time was a source of trouble to later Scottish kings. Suggesting there were Scots up here is unusual but might conform to the notion of ongoing, practical, temporary alliances between tribes from different language groups. However, his grasp of geography seems rather loose as he says the Picts and Scots then took refuge in Loch Lomond, over 100 miles (160 km) over the Scottish Highlands from Moray. Again he seems to be quoting Nennius when he tells of the 60 islands, 60 streams, 60 crags and 60 eagles in the loch. Here his enemies were supposed to have taken refuge and Arthur's men took to a fleet of boats, laid siege to the islands and starved their enemies to death. It is tempting to see in this some actual tradition as to the use of the boats by the historical Arthur and we should perhaps remember that one of the supposed 60 streams flowing into the loch was the River Douglas, where Skene located the battles on the River Dubglas. It might also be significant that one of the islands in Loch Lomond is Inchcailloch, which I have suggested might retain a name originally used of a goddess. This could have made it of some importance to the pagan religion.

However, Geoffrey was writing in Oxford and Nennius had written in north Somerset so it is understandable if their knowledge of the geography of a country neither of them ever visited should be somewhat confused. In the 600 years between these battles actually taking place and Geoffrey writing his *History* the stories of the battles appear to have flourished among the Welsh people while the P-Celtic language in Scotland seems to have gradually disappeared. This, I suggest, makes the recurring references to Scotland all the more likely to have been based on actual fact. These battles were so significant in the Arthurian traditions that they were still being talked of and even Geoffrey, a cleric writing for an aristocratic Anglo-Norman audience, ends up putting some of them in their original locations. In a clearly anachronistic fashion he has Arthur then granting lands to a variety of his followers, Moray to Urien and Lothian to Loth, whom he tells us was Arthur's brother-in-law and father of Gawain and Modred. Such an apportioning of lands by an individual would not have been likely within tribal times. The Urien mentioned might actually have been the Uruei whom we know was active in Strathclyde in the sixth century and is mentioned in *The Gododdin*. Significantly, Geoffrey also tells us that Loth was a nephew of the King of Norway. This perhaps underlines the contacts between Britain and Continental Europe, showing that the idea of the alliances of Saxons with Picts and Scots was in no way extraordinary.

Earlier we looked at Frollo, a tribune of Rome in charge of Gaul, whom Geoffrey tells us challenged Arthur to single combat to decide the day. This is certainly not the behaviour one would expect of a Roman general and is, as we have seen, the sort of behaviour we would expect from a tribal warrior. Yet again we appear to be seeing aspects of traditional tribal behaviour breaking through Geoffrey's deliberate propagandist portrayal of an idealised feudal king. Geoffrey tells us that Arthur, having received a message from Rome to go and submit himself before their justice, sent a reply saying he was coming, but at the head of an army. The numbers given for this army are fantastic in sixth-century terms, being at least 150,000 men. Even in England under Roman rule this size of army would have been impossible to raise. While he is off on this campaign he leaves his nephew Modred and his queen, Guinevere, in control of Britain. After a series of adventures and massive battles in Gaul, Arthur is just about to set off for the final push on Rome when word comes from Britain that Modred has declared himself king. He was also living 'adulterously and out of wedlock' with Queen Guinevere. There is then a curious comment in which the author declares: 'About this matter . . . Geoffrey of Monmouth prefers to say nothing.' There might be a particular reason for this unaccustomed reticence on Geoffrey's part. Modred is known to have been a Pict and there has long been discussion about the possibility of the Picts following a matrilineal succession. We know that Geoffrey is presenting us with an idealised feudal king figure, but the Arthur of the sixth century was not a king. Could Guinevere have been the possessor of sovereignty and was she in fact choosing a new king? Or is it possible that even the act of a queen effectively choosing her king (more likely a decision made by powerful interests among the Picts than a personal choice) was enough to bring the Christian warrior upon them? Could the Picts have decided to return to the practices of the pagan past and thus deliberately rejected Christianity? They had a history of this as St Patrick tells us. If Arthur was not a king but a war leader battling against paganism, we should be looking for some underlying religious reason for the battle with Modred. An interesting sidelight on this possibility comes from Gildas. Writing of the Five Tyrants he tells of Magloconus, who killed his nephew and married his widow. Gildas informs us that Magloconus had become a Christian at one point, changing from a 'raven' to a 'dove' (p. 33) but he then reverted to paganism before killing his nephew. In a very strange comment on Magloconus's marriage to his nephew's wife (p. 34), he says: 'The wedding was public, and as the lying tongues of your parasites cry (but from their lips only, not the depths of their hearts), legitimate: for she was a widow. But I call it most scandalous.' This is strange for he has already told us Magloconus had killed his own wife as well as his nephew before marrying the widow. Apart from illustrating the ongoing tension between pagan and Christian this reference to legitimacy is striking. Could Gildas be referring to some sort of legitimacy within pagan custom and belief? And could this type of idea be what caused Geoffrey to state plainly that he would prefer 'to say nothing'?

We have seen that Camlaan was considered very important, cropping up consistently in the early Welsh sources. The story at Meigle, in the heart of Pictland, does not mention Camlaan but the point of the story is clear. Vanora is punished horribly for her crime of adultery, not just put to death. Was this because the story recalls a reversion to paganism over 20 years after the Battle of Badon? This also means that Guinevere was hardly in the first flush of youth and hardly likely to have entered into the arrangement with Modred unless she had very good reason. Some support for this interpretation might be found if archaeologists ever decide to investigate her burial mound in Meigle churchyard.

In his description of the battle with Modred, Geoffrey points out that Modred had help from other pagan forces including Scots and Irish, as by this time Scotland and Ireland were distinct nation states. We are told that the struggle started at Winchester and that Guinevere went to the City of the Legions where she entered a nunnery. After a first defeat Geoffrey tells us Modred retreated towards Cornwall where Arthur caught up with him at the River Camblam. He goes on to tell us that even after Modred fell his men fought on, again suggesting this was something more than a dynastic struggle; if they were fighting to keep Modred as king, once he was dead there would seem little point. After this Arthur himself sustained a mortal wound and Geoffrey informs us he 'was carried off to the Isle of Avalon, so that his wounds might be attended to.' This seems contradictory: he was mortally wounded but was carried off to an island to be treated medically. Although Geoffrey tells us that he handed over his crown to his cousin Constantine, there is no direct mention of Arthur's death. In *The Life of Merlin*, Geoffrey elaborates this and tells us that Arthur was taken off to Avalon by Morgan and her eight sisters, whom he individually names. These nine sisters are clearly a group of pagan priestesses and are the inhabitants of the pagan magic island of Avalon. What this might mean is that Geoffrey has had access to some tradition regarding this incident that he himself cannot make much sense of. We also have the well-established Scottish practice of burying later kings on the holy island of Iona. Given the tendency of myth and legend to be presented within the known environment of the audience, do we have a location that would correspond to Iona on the east of Scotland, where we have located the Battle of Camlaan?

We have seen that there is such a location on the Isle of May, sacred to both pagans and early Christians. Its name means the Island of the Maiden(s) and intriguingly it crops up in the story of the birth of St Kentigern to Thenew, Arthur's niece. Thenew was the daughter of King Lot of the Lothians and Kentigern, as we have seen, was a significant figure in the early Scottish church. After Thenew was cast adrift by her father in a skin boat without a paddle, she drifted to the Isle of May before being taken by the tide to Culross, upriver on the north bank of the Forth. This mention of the Isle of May in the birth story of such a prestigious figure as Kentigern suggests that the place was of some considerable significance. If Arthur's body was taken out to the Isle of May to be given an honourable and prestigious burial, would this burial of a significant Christian hero provide a convenient means of taking over a previously pagan centre? This is all speculative, but might the awareness that the division between paganism and Christianity was not clear cut in Arthur's time have been enough for Geoffrey to turn away from telling us more about Guinevere's supposed adultery? As we have seen, there are grounds for seeing some level of co-existence between the two religions for a while, and this might have been embarrassing for a Christian cleric to mention.

Although Geoffrey's *History* is a propagandist work meant for an aristocratic audience, he does seem to be particularly sympathetic towards the Bretons and the Cornish. In this light it is worth remembering that the spread of Arthurian material throughout both England and France in this period has been attributed at least in part to travelling minstrels or troubadours of Breton origin. They seem to have had a considerable corpus of material dealing with the Matter of Britain, stories of love and magic, as well as knights and battles, which found a ready audience at all levels of society. Geoffrey would certainly have heard this type of material, but did he also become exposed to traditional material, handed down orally within his own family? In writing his *History of the*

Kings of Britain, Geoffrey was to some extent following the example of earlier Christian scribes who had recorded old pagan oral tales and painstakingly tried to resolve them with their own Biblically based view of the world and its history. He was taking some of the same sort of material and weaving it into a story designed to show the greatness of the English monarchy, but some of the old pagan ideas shine through. In fact, it is remarkable how much of the old ideas have survived in works that were compiled by early Christian monks in Britain and in Ireland. In this there might have been a sense of them trying to hang on to at least some of what they considered their own traditions, an idea that could be strengthened if there was a period of peaceful co-existence between the religions.

Geoffrey's vision of Arthur is that of the great overarching hero, but this is not the only version we have of Arthur from later times. In Bower's *Scotichronicon*, written in the 1440s, we are told that Arthur was illegitimate, citing Geoffrey's story of Uther Pendragon having impregnated his mother, Igraine, while magically transformed by Merlin into the shape of her husband Duke Gorlois of Cornwall. This, according to Bower, made him unfit to succeed to the throne and was the cause of the eventual battle with Modred, whom he says was a legitimate heir through his mother, Anna, Arthur's sister. Here we have another reference to inheritance through the female line. This also suggests that there were alternative views of Arthur in existence in fifteenth-century Scotland and it is possible that Bower was aware of contemporary oral material that did not see Arthur as the great Christian king, as portrayed by Geoffrey. Bower also says that Arthur, though only 15, clearly following Geoffrey, was chosen by the nobles of Britain to be their king. Here we have another clear reference to the elective aspect of leadership that we know existed among the Celtic-speaking tribal peoples of Britain.

One of the more significant contributions that Geoffrey made to the development of the modern idea of King Arthur was bringing in the figure of Merlin, the great king's wizard adviser. He had written *The Prophecies of Merlin* before his *History*, claiming to have translated another book in the British language, possibly attributed to Merlin himself. There are several early Welsh poems attributed to Merlin, whose name in Welsh was Myrddin. Merlin is said to have gone mad after the Battle of Arderydd in 573 as a result of the defeat of Gwendolau and the pagan faction, and ran off to live with the wild animals in the Forest of Celidon. Here he delivered prophecies which have survived in some of the poems attributed to him. Most modern commentators see the original Merlin, particularly the portrayal of the mad prophet in the Forest of Celidon, as based on Lailoken, a figure who occurs in Joceline's *Life of Kentigern*. Lailoken was said to have been a fool at the court of Ryderch of Strathclyde. The figure of the fool is, of course, often an ambivalent one, as much a purveyor of wisdom and insight as a jester or clown. In many so-called primitive societies, those who are mad or of singularly low intelligence are often described as being 'touched' – by God. There are suggestions that Lailoken in turn derived from an earlier figure of a Wild Man of the Woods who lived with animals. This seems to be reference to some ancient god-like or supernatural figure from the even more distant past and it is interesting that in Irish tradition there is a similarly inspired and prophetic madman. This is Suibhne Guilt, Sweeney the Wild, who flew like a bird among the treetops. This originally Scottish figure is yet another instance of a traditional tale being transplanted to Wales. This Scottish provenance is underlined by the fact that the earliest place where the name Myrddin crops up is in *The Gododdin*, where the reference is to his 'fair song', reinforcing the idea that he was a bard, or poet. It is from the various traditions concerning a poet and a prophetic madman that Geoffrey eventually created his famous figure of the wizard, the original of whom was clearly well known in sixth-century Scotland. Leo Tolstoy in his book *The Quest for Merlin* goes so far as to locate Merlin's well and cave on Hart Fell, a mountain some 15 miles (24 km) from Drumelzier, where the prophet is supposedly buried and which is close to the location of the Battle of Cat Coit Celidon.

Chapter Seven

Evidence of Pagan Locations

I HAVE SUGGESTED THAT we can see a pattern in the locations of the historical Arthur's battles as given by Nennius. Whether or not they were a series of interconnected events in a concerted campaign, there are striking similarities. Apart from the significant pagan sites near these battle sites, one is the number of these battles that are close to the site of earlier Roman occupation: the battle on the River Glen is not far from the Roman fort near Loudon Hill; the location of the battle of the River Bassas is close to the Antonine Wall; and Skene mentions a possible Roman site near Stow. The City of the Legions mentioned by Skene, whichever location one prefers, is obviously a Roman site, while the Links of Forth, suggested by Skene for the tenth battle, is not far from the Antonine Wall. This is certainly an area the Romans must have passed through on many occasions. The Battle of Agned referring probably to Edinburgh Rock has no immediate Roman locations but there are such locations a few miles both east and west at Inveresk and Cramond. The Romans must at least have been aware of any structure on Edinburgh Rock, given its location. What this shows is that the areas in which Arthur was fighting had been seen as of strategic importance by the Romans. As we know, there were no real urban sites in Scotland when the legions arrived and this continued through much of the ensuing centuries. The great majority of the Roman forts and camps could not have been built to support sieges of towns or cities. Hilltop sites like Edinburgh and Dumbarton did have some defensive function but this was not the only important function of such sites.

We should remember that the patterns of battle between different tribes are not the same as military campaigns. They are not about territorial expansion or political dominance. Raiding, endemic though it certainly was, was seasonal, and can be seen as almost formalised, though this is not to say there were no occasions of brutal slaughter. We know from later tribal times in the Scottish Highlands that there could be ongoing blood feuds of remarkable bloodthirstiness. These, however, appear to the exception rather than the norm and such raiding as did take place was generally organised to lift cattle from other tribes or clans. Such tribal warriors only ever united into large-scale forces in the face of a common threat, like invasion by an organised army, so there would be little need for the standing-army-type presence that large-scale defensive military structures require. While there probably were what would approximate to regular soldiers in such dominant hilltop sites, their presence there could just as likely hinge on the sacral import of the site as on its strategic value.

We have seen that there are notable breast-shaped mountains throughout Scotland which seem to have been the focus of religious belief, and with the existence of pagan priestess groups at specific locations such as Edinburgh, Traprain Law, Dumbarton and Stirling we should perhaps try to understand these locations as central to tribal existence in a sacral way. There is an old cliché about every stone and stream in Scotland having its own story and in a sense this reflects the direct involvement of native pagan belief with nature. The intellectual differentiation between the sacred and the profane in organised Christianity does not seem to have been matched in pagan religion. In the past such religion has often been called nature worship and this is accurate in some sense. It means an awareness of the physical environment as being inherently religious as well, and the association of so many locations in the landscape with spirits, fairies, kelpies, giants, dragons and witches shows that this involvement with the landscape was universal. In this respect the idea that a particularly shaped mountain or other geographical feature was put there deliberately by a force that not only represented but in fact *was* all life is not difficult to comprehend. If you worship a mother goddess who made the landscape and see a mountain shaped like a female breast it is not much of a leap of the imagination to see that as being a particular site of sanctity, effectively chosen for you by the selfsame goddess. This is like the practice of locating important psychological and mythological material in tales that are told within the known, and observed, landscape. It is also true that religion would not be seen in the formalised way it now functions in society. As important dates such as Beltane and Samhain were accompanied by great feasts, and as practices such as the rituals associated with hunting magic or the visiting of sacred wells for healing purposes were part of everyday life, the division between the sacred and the profane would not exist. To a great extent the sense of tribal identity which underpinned people's ideas of themselves would be intimately involved with their mythology and legends, and their landscape.

This would mean that important sites within the tribe would be more than the so-called high-status encampments of military leaders so beloved of archaeologists. Certainly the chiefs in such places had high status – you can have no higher status than chief-tainship within tribal societies, except perhaps for some religious functionaries. However, to leap from this to assuming a hierarchi-cal social structure akin to either the caste system of India or the class system of England is a leap too far. In this scenario the bat-tle sites were of extreme significance to the tribal peoples of the time and would thus present a focus for outside attack. It has long been the practice for conquering armies to try and destroy the artefacts and locations of indigenous belief. Because of the means of transmission of such belief, by word of mouth, and the subse-quent process of relating such material to the known environment this means such beliefs were, in an important sense, localised. The significant locations within such patterns of belief would be within the known environment, which does not mean to say that everything of significance had to be within constant view. People did travel, and in the Highlands of Scotland transhumance – seasonal movement of people – was practised into the eighteenth century. Though this was limited mainly to taking stock to high meadows during the summer months when food for them was abundant, it did preserve something of more ancient practices when different seasons were spent in different locales to access different food sources. This seasonal variation also made the awareness and importance of seasonal change more significant. Living in cities, as most humans now do, means that we are much less aware of seasonal and weather changes than our ancestors, who, lacking such modern advances as electric light, central heating and air-conditioning, lived much more closely with nature in the raw. This immediacy, and the need to live with such changes – and in Scotland during the winter there are only a few hours of daylight, often overcast, cold and wet – gives the belief in the forces of nature an immediacy hard for us to comprehend. Though we can perhaps envisage this type of belief as seeing the entire landscape as in some way sacred, there is no doubt that specific sites were seen as being of major importance.

Many of Scotland's mountains have tales of the Cailleach Bheara, the Hag of Winter. Most of these come from the Gaelic tradition but there are similar tales in Scots of the figure called the Gyre Carlin. Both these terms have the same meaning, the Biting Hag, and refer to her power of bringing winter onto the land. As I discuss in *The Quest for the Nine Maidens*, she and her associated priestess groups were thought to have the power of weather-working, much as later witches were believed to able to summon up winds for sailors. Now the oldest meaning of Cailleach is thought to be The Veiled One. It is this meaning that meant it became the standard word for a nun, which given the associations with ancient pagan goddess figures is somewhat ironic, and may be seen as another example of the Christianisation of the artefacts and motifs of paganism, as originally suggested by Pope Gregory to Bishop Mellitus in 609 AD. However, there is a fascinating aspect to this meaning which links directly to several of the locations of Arthur's battles and perhaps also to the Roman choice of many of their forts and marching camps. One day in Glen Clova in the southern Grampians I was watching Lochnagar, a high brooding mountain whose original name was Bein a Ciochan, the Hill of the Paps (there being two prominent breast-shaped peaks on the massif) when the weather began to change. Clouds began to drift from the west into a clear blue sky and the temperature began to fall. As the cloud cover thickened and lowered, the peaks of Lochnagar seemed to pull them down until they obscured the heights of the massif, veiling it in cloud. After a while as the temperature continued to drop, the clouds rolling round the mountain top began to spread out in a layer below the existing cloud cover and after a while the rain began. By that time I was ensconced in a local hostelry. The point here is that the mountain actually became veiled and then began to spread the weather over the landscape. It was dramatic and informative. Is this everyday behaviour pattern of our planet the reason why prominent mountains, acting as nodes of changing weather, become associated with goddesses, some of whom were known as the veiled ones? It would seem an essentially practical idea – not some mystical concept but an idea drawn from actual physical experience of the changing landscape, and the Cailleach's association with winter is just as clear. The snow falls first on the mountain tops and then spreads down into the valleys and lowlands, so the first snows, and the onset of winter, can be directly linked to the female figures associated with such mountains.

It is surely possible that this association with mountains could be linked to something similar concerning prominent hills in flat landscapes, particularly if they are breast-shaped. I have already mentioned this in relation to Dumbarton Rock, but other hills could be seen as being similar. In his fascinating book *Scottish Hill and Mountain Names*, P. Drummond tells of the *pap* or *cioch* names and also of the *mam* names of the Highlands. He says: 'Originally meaning simply a breast, it came through common use in mountain names to signify a round-topped hill of that shape. The more rounded *mam* hills are often less conically striking than the *ciochs*.' (p. 90) Within pagan thought this might mean that they represent not the protuberant breasts of the young woman but the suckling breast of the older mother figure. By this reckoning, can we see in the prominent hills of Stirling, Dumbarton, Edinburgh and Traprain a similar vestige of holiness associated with ancient pagan belief? These hilltop sites all have dedications to St Monenna, whom we have already considered in this respect. We clearly have grounds for considering that these prominent features in the landscape were the focus of pagan religious belief, even if we have little idea how such belief manifested itself other than in the tales that have survived about such places.

I am aware that this idea of the essentially sacred landscape will meet with resistance, but it is something of which I have no doubt. In recent years environmentalists have talked of Gaia, an ancient Greek goddess, as a concept for understanding the planet Earth as basically one giant interlinked being, of which we humans are but one part. Not only do I think this is a necessary antidote to the arrogant, blinkered and polluting monster that global capitalism has grown into, but it also seems to me to echo the ancient belief system I perceive as being attacked by the Christian Arthur in his battles. Time and again in Nennius, in Gildas (though he doesn't mention Arthur directly) and later in Geoffrey of Monmouth we have Arthur's opponents described as pagan. I believe at this period in the sixth century we are still dealing with a series of tribal societies in Scotland, and until the start of Northumbrian expansionism in the following century the idea of the nation state or petty kingdom has not yet taken root, though as we shall see this was perhaps preceded by something of the same idea in Dalriada. I would go further and suggest that in the concerted campaign of Arthur's battles we see the Christian church taking on a political role that effectively laid the path towards greater centralisation and the growth of such states. In this St Columba, a generation after the accepted dates for Arthur, seems to have played a major role.

If Arthur were indeed attempting to supplant pagan beliefs with Christianity this would give good grounds for him surviving as a heroic figure in an increasingly Christianised island. Behind that Christian figure, however, several writers have seen what they think is an ancient god. Lewis Spence in *The Magic Arts in Celtic Britain*, a highly speculative but informative work, tells us that the story of Arthur is like that of the Egyptian god Horus, son of Osiris – both have companies of warriors dedicated to slaying monsters, both visit the Underworld – and Spence goes on to link the story of the Grail to the mythic story of the Nile (p. 155). Interestingly, he tells us of 'the cavern of Querti, shaped like two breasts, from which arose the sacred flood that blessed the land.' (ibid) Other commentators have compared the Arthurian material to the story of Adonis, a Syrian god who descended annually into Hades, just as Arthur descended to Annwn, the clear implication being that as a god figure, Arthur came to the British Isles from the Near East. Other commentators have seen Arthur as a bear god, in some way linked to the Great Bear constellation in the sky, and Paul Screeton in *Quicksilver Heritage* (p. 54) pointed out that among the hundreds of Arthurian place names in the British Isles many of them are applied to Megalithic and other very early sacred sites, some of which feature supposedly significant astronomical alignments. The poet Robert Graves in *The White Goddess* saw Arthur as being a form of an earlier god Bran. One of the meanings of Bran, Graves tells us (p. 51), is 'crow', and Spence wrote: 'And

Horus took the shape of a hawk, as did Arthur that of a raven or crow. Moreover, the name of Arthur's nephew Gwalchmei means 'hawk' while his sister Morgan is probably the Morrigan, or crow-goddess, of Irish mythology.' (p. 155) This association with the crow, a carrion eater, is specifically linked to the Morrigan who visits the battlefield in the shape of a crow. There is perhaps a link to ancient Norse belief here for Odin had two magic crows, Thummin and Mummin, and he had handmaidens who visited the battlefields to select those among the fallen worthy of entering the warriors' paradise of Valhalla. T. W. Rolleston in his *Celtic Myths and Legends* (p. 138) saw Valhalla as being related to Avalon: 'Avalon, a word which seems to imply some kind of fairyland, a Land of the Dead, and may be related to the Norse Valhalla. It was not until later times that Avalon came to be identified with an actual site in Britain (Glastonbury).' Also, Odin's battle maidens, the Valkyrie, were in several instances said to number nine, just like Morgan and her sisters of Avalon. Classically trained scholars will, of course, trace the British and Norse mythic ideas back to the Mediterranean, but we should always remember that contact is a two-way process and that Scotland had Maes Howe and many other staggering Megalithic structures before the Egyptians raised their pyramids. Arthur's descent into the Underworld after the magical cauldron has been extensively commented on and there are similar ideas in the mythologies of many different parts of the world, not just the Mediterranean.

One of the most remarkable ideas to be associated with Arthurian traditions is that of the Holy Grail. From the twelfth century onwards the belief was that the Holy Grail was the cup of the Christian Last Supper and also the receptacle said to have been used by Joseph of Arimathea to catch the blood of the crucified Christ. Late Arthurian romance has several heroes setting out on the quest to find this most holy of Christian relics. Referring to Chretien de Troyes' *Conte de Grall* in his own *Celtic Myth and*

Arthurian Romance (p. 140), R. S. Loomis tells us: 'Throughout the romances of this cycle . . . glimmerings of seasonal myth, of phallic ritual, of Celtic vessels of plenty, of divine weapons, can be spied here and there.' One of the greatest Arthurian heroes intimately involved with the Grail Quest is Galahad. Loomis mentions that one of his ancestors is a certain Celidione. He further tell us that Merlin, the wizard companion of Arthur in so many romances, was known as Merlin Celidonius, which arose from his having prophesied in the Caledonian Forest. Even if the reference is not to Merlin it seems clear it must be to the Caledonian Forest in some way. I do not intend to investigate Merlin here, suffice it to say he seems to have been based initially on Lailoken whose story occurs in *Life of Kentigern*. This is set in Strathclyde in the latter half of the sixth century and thus not contemporary with Arthur, at least as far as the evidence so far presented is concerned. What is significant here is that here we have one of the greatest of the Arthurian heroes being descended from someone who can obviously be associated with southern Scotland. Loomis saw Merlin along with many other figures in Arthurian romance as having originated as gods amongst the Welsh people. I do not want here to begin to analyse the later romances but it is surely of some importance that we have a reference to Scotland surviving after more than half a millennium and cropping up in a French text. This is a clear example of the fact that the Gwr Y Gogledd, the Men of the North, took their traditions with them when they moved to Wales from central and southern Scotland. And among those traditions were tales concerning what is surely the original motif from which the Grail developed, the magic cauldrons that occur in several instances.

The cauldron which Arthur seeks in Annwn, the Underworld, is, according to the Taliesin poem *Prideu Annwn* (*The Spoils of Annwn*), to be kept warm by the breath of nine maidens and was encrusted with pearls. It is the cauldron of poetry and inspiration of the Welsh goddess Cerridwen. It also corresponds to other magical cauldrons in both Welsh and Irish sources. In the tale of Peredur, son of Efrawg, there is the magical cauldron of Bendigeidfran, in which if a dead warrior is bathed he will be brought back to life. Bendigeidfran is another name for the god Bran with whom we have seen a suggested connection to Arthur. A similar vessel crops up in Irish tradition – the Cauldron of the Dagda, the father of the gods in Irish mythology. It would also feed a multitude, nine at a time, but would not boil the food of a coward. Warriors restored to life by Dagda's cauldron could go back into battle but were mute – they could not talk of what they had seen in the other world. Clearly this is a significant motif amongst both the P- and Q-Celtic-speaking peoples. Markale in *Women of the Celts* discusses the link between these magical cauldrons and the idea of the Christian Grail and makes an important point when he says: 'We can . . . conclude that the Grail, whatever shape the texts give it, is a feminine symbol, and that the quest that the knight undertakes is a search for femininity.' (p. 174) There are several representations of the cauldron on these remarkable monuments the Pictish Symbol Stones, and one, on the Glamis Manse stone, has two pairs of legs sticking out of it. This has been interpreted locally as some form of ritual drowning but I would suggest it is probably a reference to the cauldron of Bendigeidfran or something similar within Pictish tradition. In the light of the pagan beliefs we are considering there is another notable cauldron. This is a big iron cauldron found among the clearly votive deposits from Carlingwark Loch in the Scottish Borders, currently on display in the new Museum of Scotland in Edinburgh. These offerings to what I see as a goddess – Carling-wark is a name derived from the Carlin who corresponds in Scots tales to the Cailleach of Gaelic tradition – are from an earlier period. In the light of such votive offerings we should perhaps recall Malory's tale of Sir Bedevere returning Excalibur to the Lady of the Lake, a story that has local variants from the Borders to Cornwall. Intriguingly, 7 miles (11 km) north-east of Calringwark Loch is Loch Arthur.

We know that water was venerated in pagan religion and that many Scottish wells in particular were the location of specific rites, some into the twentieth century and at least one, the Cloutie Well on the Black Isle in the north of Scotland, has never stopped being the site of offerings. In trying to discern what remains from the pagan religion I have spent many years looking at the Scottish landscape and there is one site that has long seemed to be of particular importance.

McArthur and the Goddess

A couple of years ago I was phoned by a Glaswegian called Hugh McArthur, who is deeply interested in the origin of the McArthur clan. An Old Gaelic saying has it, in translation: 'There is nothing older than the hills/MacArthur and the Devil.' This is probably a Christianised version of something older and there are those who believe that the MacArthurs were originally the dominant group, or clan, or tribe in Argyll before the rise of the Campbells. Hugh told me that he believed that the Taliesin poem *Spoils of Annwn* described an actual battle, an assault by the Christian Arthur on what can be understood as the Mother Church of paganism. I have to admit I was dubious and told him that unless he could locate that Mother Church in one specific location I did not see much merit in his idea. The location he told me was the one, the only, place in Scotland that I was prepared to accept could have been of this level of importance in the pagan religion. This is the Corryvreckan whirlpool between the Inner Hebridean islands of Scarba and Jura.

This remarkable place is the site of one of the most dramatic geophysical events on our planet and yet is today really known only to the sailors and inshore fishermen who sail the beautiful waters of the Firth of Lorne. One of only seven major whirlpools on the surface of our planet, the Corryvreckan, is formed by a remarkable confluence of tides that impel the Atlantic waters through the Gulf of Corryvreckan and out into the advancing force of the Atlantic tide. For most of every day the waters surge round Scarba and Jura and twirl round an underwater spike just off the southern shore of Scarba which is called the Cailleach. To this day the whirlpools formed here and thrown into the advancing Atlantic are known among Gaelic storytellers as 'the breath of the goddess under the waters'. There are a couple of stories of how the Corry-vreckan got its name and the oldest is quite remarkable. In this tale the name means simply the Cauldron of the Plaid, *breacan* being Gaelic for the plaid, the traditional one-piece tartan garment of the Highlands that gave rise to the modern kilt. It was here in this whirlpool that the Cailleach Bheur, our Hag of Winter, came from her home on Ben Nevis, the highest mountain in the British Isles, to wash her plaid at the beginning of winter. This washing is how the Corryvreckan, at its wildest at the beginning of winter when the tides are at their strongest, can be heard over 30 miles (48 km) away on the islands of the Outer Hebrides. Once she has washed her plaid, the Cailleach spreads it out to dry over the Mamore mountains. Because she is the oldest creature, the first born of the world, her plaid is white and this is how the first snowfall of winter arrives. To watch the Corryvreckan, even on a calm and sunny autumn day, is to feel wonder and sense mystery. From a flat calm sea a wave erupts and booms out over the sea as the whirlpool forms. The spiral turns and as it goes off and eventually dissipates in the Atlantic tide, another forms, and then another, and then another, on and on.

This clockwise spiral is to be seen on carved stones at the ancient Megalithic structure of New Grange in Ireland, raised around 3500 BC, and on many cup-marked stones throughout the British Isles. It seems to form part of the spiral snake designs of some Pictish Symbol Stones. Perhaps a reference to it may be seen in the spiral and sword motif from Östergötland in Sweden dating from around 1500 BC. In this circular spiral, interpreted by some as a sun symbol, and the sword it is possible to discern the female and male principles, just as can be seen in the Corryvreckan itself in the motif of the whirlpool as a cauldron and the stone pillar below the waves. It might not stretch a point to see a link to the spiral motifs of Maltese and other Mediterranean art of thousands of years ago. In *Facing the Ocean* Professor Barry Cunliffe has outlined the ongoing cultural and economic links between divergent societies up and down the eastern Atlantic coast from Morocco to the islands north of Scotland, and even beyond. People travelling in their ships up or down the west coast of Scotland would hear of this marvel, particularly if the whirlpool was associated with the Mother Goddess of ancient belief. In 1934 J. G. Mackay wrote 'The Deer Cult and the Deer-Goddess Cult of the Ancient Caledonians'. In this he noted the association of deer with the Cailleach in many traditional tales, concluding there was a definite cult of the Deer Goddess. This suggestion has been rejected by some but there is supporting evidence. On several Pictish Symbol Stones, including the Glamis Manse stone, there are deer heads, which are inscribed in such a way as to suggest masks rather than simply severed heads. On one stone, Rhynie No. 5, there is what could be interpreted as a shirt and head mask combined, an idea that receives remarkable support from a passage in the Gaelic tale *The Widow's Son* in Campbell's *Popular Tales of the West Highlands* (1 pp. 62f.). Here the hero goes out to shoot a deer and the first time he raises his gun the deer has a woman's face, the next time it is a woman to the waist, and the third time he is faced with a beautiful young woman. This seems to me to be a description of a deer priestess taking off her costume. As I have said before, the weight of evidence is important in determining proof, for we can hardly find witnesses to such ancient belief today.

A suggestion made in a television programme a few years ago is a case in point. A diviner called Donovan who spent a great deal of time out on the moors said that he dowsed the same patterns under deer-rutting stands as under stone circles. Did the builders of the circles raise their stones because they saw the deer mate and thus associated the place with fertility? Or did they respond in some way to the same unseen forces that the deer responded to? We also know that deer have been seen as a symbol of rebirth and fertility because they cast off their horns and grow new ones each year. M. Gimbutas showed the extent of horned altars in third and fourth millennium BC Balkan countries in *The Goddesses and Gods of Ancient Europe*. This might tie in because the island to the south of the Corryvreckan is Jura, derived from the Norse meaning Deer Isle. It is tempting to see some similarity between the traditional tale of the Cailleach and the Corryvreckan and the idea of Hvergelmer, the Roaring Cauldron, of Norse mythology which equates with the Sea Mill, operated by nine sea maidens, that grinds out the physical universe from the bodies of the Ice Giant Ymir, slain by the gods at the start of our world. There is also a reference to the World Spike at the centre of the Mill in this tale which is again very like the stone spike of the Corryvreckan. There are other motifs associated with the Corryvreckan that underline this notion of ancient sanctity and there is the remarkable tale from Jura that has echoes both of Arthurian stories and the nine maidens. This is the story of Mac Iain Direach who is sent on a magic quest to find a blue feather from a specific bird. As is normal in many such quest tales he has to get a number of magical objects to help him in his quest. One of these is the Glaibh Soluis, the Sword of Light which is in the possession of the Seven Big Women of Jura, who are clearly supernatural beings and are akin to many Nine Maidens groups. This is reminiscent of Arthur and his magic sword Excalibur and the association with Morgan and her sisters, likewise living on an island.

All of this material associated with the Corryvreckan area certainly suggests that it was seen as a site of sanctity in the far past. It is only recently that scientists have become aware that the Earth's oceans also have whirlpools – giant eddies that can measure over 20 kilometres across. They circulate warm, plankton-bearing flows of water into the depths of the ocean, effectively seeding it. This corresponds very closely to the idea of the life-giving cauldron of the Mother Goddess. The Corryvreckan is the most stunning geophysical event in Europe and one of the wonders of the world, yet it is little known. Why? Perhaps the reason is precisely because it was a site of such pagan importance that it had to be kept hidden by the dominant religion of Christianity. Later tales of the Corryvreckan tend to concentrate on how dangerous it is, but unless caught by bad weather no local sailor would be foolish enough to be caught in it, and when the tide is slack it is possible to sail safely through the Gulf of the Corryvreckan. The fact is that to this day this is one of the most popular sailing areas in European waters.

There is a tradition in Scotland that in fact this stunning whirlpool got its name from a whirlpool off Rathlin Island just off the north coast of Ireland. This is in fact a rip tide effect and is in no way as remarkable as the Corryvreckan, though it has long been known as a danger to shipping. It was thought that Gaelic originated in Ireland and came to Scotland only in 500 AD, and because more early Irish texts survive than Scottish texts, either in Gaelic or Scots, that cultural influence had to run from Ireland to Scotland. This is an idea that does not stand much scrutiny, however, as we know the people living in western Scotland and northern Ireland have been in touch, by sea, since before Megalithic times. It does not even have to be a particularly good day to see Scotland from Ulster or vice versa. If people were travelling up and down the eastern coast of the Atlantic five thousand years ago it is perfectly obvious that areas like Galloway, Kintyre and Ulster would have been in regular contact. The Hebridean people are even today known for being great sea travellers and the fact that some of them still call the Corryvreckan whirlpool 'the breath of the goddess under the waves' suggests they have never forgotten it entirely. I suggest here that the idea of the Corryvreckan in Scotland being named after a less dramatic one in Ireland is in fact an attempt to suppress the knowledge of the former because of its pagan significance. The Corryvreckan turns up in the story of one particular figure that Hugh McArthur, like some others before him, sees as being contemporary with the original historical Arthur.

St Columba and the Corryvreckan

Columba, as we have already seen, was a very political kind of churchman. His expulsion from Ireland was as a result of the Battle of Cul Drebene which he started by refusing to accept the judgement of a religious court concerning a psalter he had copied without its owner's permission. He came to Scotland to the already sacred island of Iona. We do not know exactly how Columba managed to obtain Iona and I would suggest that the idea that he could have been given it by a 'king' as early as 563 is not very likely. As we have seen, Scotland was as yet not composed of kingdoms, even in the west among the Gaelic-speaking peoples of Dalriada. In *Life of St Columba*, Adomnan (p. 118) tells us:

> Likewise, another day, while St Columba was in his mother church, he suddenly smiled and called out: 'Colman mac Beognai has set sail to come here, and is now in great danger in the surging tides of the whirlpool of Corryvreckan. Sitting in the prow, he lifts up his hands to heaven and blesses the turbulent, terrible sea. Yet the Lord terrifies him in this way, not so the ship in which he sits should be overwhelmed by the waves, but rather to rouse him to pray more fervently that he may sail through the peril and reach us here.'

This is, I believe, a reference to the Corryvreckan between Scarba and Jura. At the time Adomnan wrote his *Life of St Columba* in the early years of the seventh century there can be little doubt that Christianity had not eradicated paganism amongst the people of Scotland. It would therefore make sense for him to include something that would make the point about the supremacy of Christianity, and the power of prayer over the ancient powers of paganism. Sailing to Iona from Ireland one would pass the Gulf of Corryvreckan at a distance of no more than a few miles. What we know of contemporary seamanship, although it was of a high standard, suggests it is likely for safety reasons, particularly in skin boats, that many journeys would stay close to shore, bringing travellers closer to the Corryvreckan with the consequent risk of being blown off course and closer to the whirlpool by bad weather.

I believe that the existence of the Corryvreckan and the widespread use of the spiral in early religious design are linked as an expression of fundamental mythology – the explanation of the physical world and its attributes. We know that the Cailleach, like similar creatures in Welsh tradition, was said to have created the landscape, particularly the Hebrides which are supposed to have been formed when she dropped her apron full of building material meant for elsewhere. This shows her to have been the focus of creation mythology and her relationship to the Corryvreckan would make this a very sacred spot indeed. Whether Arthur and his companions, after having fought a series of battles near other sites of pagan importance in central Scotland, would then plan an assault on a site here is at the very least an interesting theory. We have already seen there is a suggestion that at least one of the sites associated with Arthur was on the Rhinns of Galloway, only a few miles from Ulster and a perfect location for sailing northwards. The islands off the west coast of Scotland were in medieval times the location of the Lordship of the Isles, a society known as Gall-Gael – the Gall part referring to the Germanic-speaking Norsemen and the Gael to the Gaelic speakers. This was an area independent of Scotland as a whole and it is at least possible that this and the earlier alliances and political groupings formed by the incoming Vikings of the ninth century could have been preceded by something similar among the tribespeople who inhabited the coasts and islands of the area.

One of the classic Scots ballads collected by the great song-collector F. J. Child known as *The Queen of Scotland* (Child 301) has been seen by some scholars as deriving from Arthurian tradition. It is similar to the story of Carados in *Perceval*, the French romance written by Chretien de Troyes around 1190. In the ballad the hero is threatened by a serpent which wraps itself around him. A passing maiden lets the serpent bite off her breast and the serpent lets the hero go. Her wound soon heals and she and the hero are married. Soon after that she gives birth to a son and her breast grows back. In the late nineteenth century a tale collected in Argyll from a Gaelic speaker by J. F. Campbell tells a similar story. In this story the daughter of a wise woman falls in love with the son of the king of Ireland despite warnings from her mother. The prince has been put under a spell by his stepmother which turns his shirt into a serpent. The prince is put into a cauldron of herbs and the serpent springs out and fastens on to the girl's breast which has to be cut off by her mother. Her breast is replaced with a breast made of gold after which she marries the prince. A later and somewhat different version of the story was gathered in the 1970s. It has been suggested that this story came into Scotland from France but it is just as likely to have survived here from an early date and been transported to France. After all, as Adomnan noted in the seventh century there was trade between the two areas in his lifetime. It is difficult to discern what lay behind this mysterious story and it seems in its use of the serpent and sacrifice motifs to hint at something pagan and the placing of the prince in the cauldron certainly suggests it. What is telling is that it has survived in both of Scotland's indigenous languages, once as song and once as story. Could they both have arisen from an original P-Celtic version? P-

Celtic was spoken alongside Gaelic back in the sixth century and, in the form of Pictish, used to be spoken in many eastern areas where Scots has long been the everyday speech of the locals.

Linda Gowans in her article 'Arthurian Survivals in Scottish Gaelic' (p. 48) makes the point that the name of the hero in the Gaelic version of the tale is Sior Bhiolodh, Sheen Billy, a well known referent to Gawain. The best known of the stories regarding this hero is *Gawain and the Green Knight* which has been interpreted as basically pagan. We do not have any great corpus of Arthurian tales surviving in Scottish Gaelic, though I have suggested some strong similarities in the story of Mac Iain Direach. Linda Gowans also mentions four other Gaelic tales, the best known of which is *Am Bron Binn*, in which the hero is Gawain. To date most consideration of these has seen them as coming into Scottish Gaelic no earlier than the medieval period and I am unaware of any such material linked to specific locales in Gaelic.

Chapter Eight

Artair mac Aedan and Columba

IN THE PRECEDING CHAPTER we looked at the rhyme concerning the MacArthur clan of Argyll. There has long been a tradition within the clan that they were descended from Smervie Mor, the son of King Arthur, mentioned earlier. According to the Campbell tradition, Smervie was known as the fool of the forest, which suggests links to Peredur in *The Mabinogion*, who is roughly raised in the forest away from Arthur's court, and also with Merlin in his aspect of the Wild Man of the Woods. Another version has it that they are descended from Artair son of Aedan Mac Gabhran, 'king' of the Scots of Dalriada, who is mentioned in Adomnan's *Life of St Columba*. This Artair's mother was said to have been a princess from among the Britons of Strathclyde which would conform to what seems to have been the general pattern – that the various tribes or peoples of sixth century Scotland were in close and regular contact. There are those who see this Artair mac Aedan as being the original Arthur. The reasoning is that here we have an attested historical character in the right area and in the right century. This would make Arthur a contemporary of St Columba, but the Battle of Camlaan, mentioned in the Welsh Annals as happening in 537, more likely 539, would have to have happened some 40 years later.

THE BATTLE OF ARDERYDD

That the struggle between paganism and Christianity was ongoing is shown by the Battle of Arderydd which took place in 573 according to the Welsh Annals and was fought between the pagan

Gwendolau and three leading chiefs whom Skene believed went on to found kingdoms: Melgwynn of Gwuynedd, Rydderch Hael of Strathclyde and Aedan Mac Gabhran of Dalriada. This makes sense in the scenario I have been suggesting: that we are dealing with a tribal society beginning to move towards the creation of nation states, though whether we can consider these individuals as in any way like later feudal kings is dubious. The Battle of Arderydd is also the battle where Merlin is said, in Welsh tradition, to have gone mad. This episode seems to be based on an episode in the *Life of Kentigern* where one Lailoken goes mad after the battle and retreats to the Caledonian Forest. St Kentigern is himself a rather mysterious figure whose mother, being the daughter of Lot of the Lothians, was Arthur's niece. What is clear is that another battle fought in the north, at Arthuret near Carlisle but over the Scottish border, also became an important part of Welsh tradition, occurring in The Welsh Triads and in *The Mabinogion*. It is a clear example of the transplanted traditions of the Gwr Y Gogledd moving to Wales. The battle took place ten years after the arrival of St Columba in Scotland and was fought near modern Carwinelow, a place name derived from Caer Gwendolau, the seat, or perhaps castle, of Gwendolau.

This battle is also significant in that it has come down to us as a clear defeat of a pagan leader by a combined force of Christians. The move from tribalism towards the later developing kingdoms could well have been influenced by what I have suggested was behind the battles of Arthur – the struggle between Christianity and paganism. We have so little in the way of historical material dating to the early sixth century that it is tempting to try and understand the period by what we know was happening 40 and 50 years later. In this respect the figure of St Columba looms large, mainly because we have Adomnan's *Life of St Columba*, written around 690, though there are other Irish texts referring to him. We have to remember that this was almost exactly 100 years after

Columba's death and that Adomnan was also the Abbot of Iona. He therefore had an interest in presenting Columba in as favourable a light as possible. Columba was expelled from Ireland and in order to re-establish his reputation we can be sure he would want to be considered successful by his peers in his new location. Adomnan tells us he arrived in Scotland in 563. The story as presented by Adomnan has Columba making prophecies and defeating wizards who resisted Christianity. We should remember that there are examples of Christian martyrs from an early period in Scotland, showing that there was no gradual and inexorable gentle spread of the new word of God amongst the pagans, as some church historians have suggested. There are also some curious incidents in Columba's story, at least to the modern reader, including the burying alive of the monk Oran on arrival at Iona. He was dug up three days later and re-buried on Columba's orders when he began to talk of his experiences. Columba was also a bard and in what seems a veiled reference to Druidism said he feared nothing more than the sound of an axe in the 'oak groves of Derry'. This seems to be a reference to a nemeton or pagan sacred site, the oak having been seen as important in pagan religion over a very wide area, and elsewhere Columba referred to Christ as his 'Druid'. The sound of an axe in the groves of Derry reads as if it might be an allusion to the destruction of a pagan religious site and the passing away of the Old Religion. Again we have a strange sense of there being some kind of co-existence between Christianity and paganism, here in the mouth of the most famous of the Scottish saints. The monk Joceline, in *Life of Kentigern*, said that he converted many who had lapsed into apostasy, that is, turned away from Christianity, some of them having done so twice. This presents us with a picture of a volatile situation between Christian and pagan up to the dawn of the seventh century at least.

We know that Columba was instrumental in pushing Aedan Mac Gabhran to the fore in Dalriada. In Adomnan's *Life of St*

Columba the story is that Columba was visited in a dream by an angel, who struck the saint with a scourge because he thought Aedan's brother Eoganan was more suited to be leader (pp. 208f.). This happened on three successive nights after which, Adomnan tells us, Columba carried the scar of the angel's whip for the rest of his life. He then ordained Aedan as king. Whether Columba had such power through his own dynastic connections in Ireland or because of his religious position is not clear at this distance but it does show the extent of his political influence. It is this Aedan's son Artair who it has been suggested was the original hero. There seems to be no doubt that Aedan would have been an active proponent of Christianity and Skene's citing of his presence at the fateful Battle of Arderydd makes this clear. It is feasible that it was his Christianity that led to him having Columba's support. The cleric was on a mission to convert wholesale numbers of pagans to the new religion to make up for the good Christians killed at the fateful Battle of Cul Drebene. What better way than to enlist the help of the local chief or over chief of Dalriada? My reluctance to use the word king is simply because it leads to all the assumptions that have accrued with regards to the term over the centuries since Aedan's time. The tribe itself, or the warriors therein, would traditionally have selected the fittest and most able to lead them in battle and it is tempting to see Columba as taking over this function himself and promoting someone who would lead the warriors best, in spreading the Word of Christ. If the Dalriadans were Christians by the time he arrived this might have been exactly how he operated.

In terms of his influence as a chief, and Aedan does seem to have been the over chief of the four branches of the Dalriadan Scots, he would have been as influential as a king in many ways. It is therefore tempting to see Columba trying to develop a political structure alongside his new church – a structure that would help him in his mission to convert the pagan Picts. Aedan eventually

died in 608, five years after a decisive defeat at the Battle of
Degastan, modern Dawston in Liddesdale, at the hands of an
Anglian army under the leadership of Ethelfrith, known to his
contemporaries as The Twister. Amongst Aedan's allies were men
from Ireland, and though the Anglians sustained heavy losses they
were victorious. Suggestions have been made that Aedan may have
been called in to help the Gododdin against the Angles, and
though the latter were still mainly pagan at this stage, we can possibly see in Ethelfrith's actions the expansionism of a social structure becoming more like a proto-kingdom than a purely tribal
society. The situation remained volatile for centuries to come, first
due to Northumbrian expansion and subsequently as the various
nation states of north Britain began to be forged. Not until the
ninth century and the accession of Kenneth MacAlpin to the combined leadership of the Scots and Picts do things really begin to
stabilise. Even then, for many centuries, due to dynastic struggle,
problems with the Highland and Border clans, and resistance to
English attempts at conquest, Scotland was rarely peaceful for
extended periods. It is in this period of the early seventh century
that Manau Gododdin begins to come under severe external stress
and 30 years later Edinburgh itself was besieged. Things were
changing. Even if Ethelfrith and his Anglian people were pagan,
Bede tells us that Edwin of Northumbria (617–33) was accepted
into the Christian church and thereafter Christianity seems to have
become dominant throughout northern Britain. By 664 we have
the Synod at Whitby where the Roman and Celtic version of the
Christian faith met to the latter's permanent disadvantage.

The loyalty to the church, even with as localised a structure as
the Columban church had, would tend to diminish the strength of
the kinship ties that were integral to the tribal system. As we have
seen, the pagan religion (and there are grounds for suggesting that
the pagans would not have been aware of a religion as separate
from other aspects of their life) was very much localised in the

landscape and effectively each tribe would have its own religion. Even if their beliefs and rituals were exactly the same as those of neighbouring tribes they would be set round their own family groups and within their own environment. An example of this can be seen in eighteenth- and nineteenth-century reports of the Beltane fires in Scotland where it seems as if virtually every parish had its own fire site. There were additional major fire sites, as we have seen, on places like Tinto Hill. This is surely a local aspect of previous universal pagan belief. We can perhaps understand such localised rites as helping to preserve the close family ties of rights and responsibilities that were necessary to keep the tribal system together. Once there is loyalty to something outside the tribe such ties are inevitably weakened. Whereas before the men of the tribe would unite as warriors for raiding purposes or in defence of their lands and possessions, now there was something else that could lead to the call to arms. The new religion with its officiants no longer an integral part of the tribe was perhaps perceived as a direct assault not just on ancient beliefs but on traditional tribal practice. The role of Arthur as a leader of a Christian war band can be seen as absolutely central in this. He is calling on other warriors to fight, not for the tribe and their kin, but out of loyalty to a new religion. This model would also make sense if what we are seeing in the sixth century is a contemporary warrior taking the name of a legendary or even mythological hero in an attempt to rally support for his activities. He would be bringing the tribes together in traditional fashion in fact to institute a revolutionary change in the tribes themselves. It is this weakening of the tribal ties and the consequent importance of the Christian church that I would suggest is the trigger for the move away from pure tribalism towards the creation of the nation state, complete with kings and centralised courts with the Christian clerics in constant attendance at such centres of power. Such courts were centralised in function, not necessarily in locale, for even when Scotland as a whole became a nation it was customary for many generations that the court would travel around the country. Previous to the establishment of the monasteries there would have been no cohesive organisation within the pagan religion that could serve as a counterbalance to tribal interests. It is remarkable, however, that certain of the traditional aspects of tribal warrior society, like inter-tribal cattle-raiding, continued in the Highland areas for more than another millennium. This must in part be due to the geography of the Highlands which saw the population continuing to live in separate territories defined primarily by the river valleys, or glens, that pierce the mountains. To return to Columba – is he manipulating the tribal system in Dalriada towards something more like a modern nation state to further the Christian cause, and his own interests?

It seems certain that Aedan's sons, Artair and Eochaid Finn, would, like their father, be Christians. Adomnan tell us that these two fell in battle as foretold by the saint. This is said to have been in battle with the Miathi, a battle in which Aedan was himself present and which probably occurred in the latter years of the sixth century. Adomnan does not tell us that the Miathi were pagan though he does refer to them as barbarians which might mean the same thing. It has been suggested that Adomnan might have meant non-Gaelic-speakers by this term but this would seem particularly harsh in the light of what we have seen were the relationships between the different language groups in Scotland at the time. Certainly there were battles between these groups but as raiding and battle appear to have been endemic within the separate language groups this proves nothing. In the Dalriadans' battle with the Miathi are we seeing the same sort of activity I suggest Arthur was involved in – battle with pagans? These Miathi are thought to have been the same people mentioned by the Greek writer Dio Cassius in the second century as the Maetae, whom he called one of the two divisions of the northern peoples, the other being the

Caledonians. Suggestions have been made that their lands incorporated the Hill of Dumyat (Dun Maetae in the Ochil Hills near Stirling) and Myot Hill in the south-eastern corner of the Kilsyth Hills. These two locations, both with what are interpreted as hillforts, are only 12 miles (19 km) apart and overlook the southern approaches of the Gap of Stirling.

Here we are very much in the area I have suggested for some of the battles attributed to Arthur by Nennius. Two other place names to the east of these, about the same distance apart, have been interpreted as referring to the Gododdin: Clackmannan on the north of the River Forth and Slamannan, on the moors to the south of the river overlooking the Falkirk area. However, Adomnan tells us that the Miathi were 'turned in flight' which could suggest that they had in fact come in to the area of the Gap of Stirling, perhaps from further north in Pictland. They were after all referred to earlier as one of the main divisions of the Picts. If they were from elsewhere why do we have Dumyat and Myot Hill? Could this Fort of the Maetae correspond to Rathillet, the Fort of the Ulsterman in northern Fife, a name perhaps referring to some sort of temporary visit by tribes from another area as part of some alliance? Within the area of the Picts there are quite a few place names including Scot, like Scotstoun, and even a few that have Inglis or English in them. As we have seen that tribal alliances had been constant over several centuries, perhaps such names reflect consequent temporary or even medium-term settlement by other tribes, or perhaps their warriors, in such locations. Adomnan tells us that Artair fell in this battle with his brother Eochaid Finn but we do not know where this battle took place. It certainly seems to have been a battle between Christian and pagan and it has been suggested that this is the battle referred to in Irish annals for 582/3 as the Battle of Manu.

MOUNT BANNAWG

The Kilsyth and Campsie Hills which run west from the Gap of Stirling have been interpreted as Mount Bannawg, mentioned in several Welsh sources which McQueen has suggested as the boundary between Strathclyde and the Pictish territory of Fortriu. Here we are very much in the debatable lands of Scotland and if the suggestions from place names are correct we have here the different tribes of Miathi/Maetae and Gododdin living on virtually the same territory at the same time. The Gododdin are in existence, as the Votadini, at the time Ptolemy, the Greek geographer, drew his map of Britain at the close of the first century, up until at least the dawn of the seventh century, and we have the Miathi/Maetae mentioned at the close of the second century AD and again by Adomnan at the close of the seventh century. This is certainly confusing but might be interpreted as tribal arrangements being much more fluid than has been realised. It is also true that Ptolemy, coming from Greece where the city state was the norm would have not been in the best position to give a coherent analysis of a complex and probably dynamic situation. The idea of the peoples of northern Britain being divided into two main groups occurs again and again. First we have the Maetae and the Caledonians in the second century, then the Dicalydones and the Verturiones in the fourth century followed by the idea of the southern and northern Picts in the sixth century. All of this is, of course, coming from outside the area under consideration and it might help us to think of this division as being not between two peoples but between two tribal confederations. Again the late survival of so many different clans in the Scottish Highlands might give us a better model for analysis than the notion of two peoples living in some kind of centralised fashion. Within this it still seems hardly likely that the Gododdin and the Maetae could occupy the same space but we should remember that where different tribes or peoples come up against each other there are often areas of mutual interdependence. Professor Sandy Fenton of the Scottish Ethnological Archive made a telling point in this regard. At a conference a few years ago he attacked the idea of the Highland Line. This is the notion that the Highland fault, the line of mountains and glens that runs south-west to north-east across Scotland from the Trossachs to near Stonehaven, was the dividing line between two distinct societies. Professor Fenton suggested we might be better thinking of it as a Highland sausage – an indeterminate area of communality between two different language groups and/or societies.

With easy access into the area of the Gap of Stirling by water, up and down the Forth and Allan waters, and relatively straightforward passage to the west – even Dumbarton is only 30 miles (48 km) or so to the west – this would obviously be an area where different peoples would meet. We know of Britons, Picts, Gododdin, Scots, Maetae and Saxons in this area over just a couple of centuries. Recently economic historians have even been considering whether the Antonine Wall itself might have been to protect trade routes rather than to stop wholesale invasion from more northern tribes, providing a line of safe communication in a highly volatile area. Again the fact that Slamannan and Clackmannan are on opposite sides of the Wall suggests at least that it does not follow the traditional boundary between different tribes. And if the tribes to the north of the Forth–Clyde line sometimes banded together why should it be different south of that line? As already noted, the placing of the Caledon wood south of the Forth–Clyde line might even suggest that all of Scotland can be interpreted as being occupied by the Caledonians, whom some Roman authors saw as being Picts.

Bede's statement that there were five languages spoken in Britain – Gaelic, British, Pictish, English and Latin – has led to a situation where too much effort has gone into trying to tie down the various peoples living in Dark Age Scotland by what language they spoke. If what we are seeing is a succession of different P-

Celtic-speaking warrior tribes, perhaps trying to separate them out is impossible. The Picts are nowadays accepted to have been north of the Forth–Clyde line but this is only a line on the map and has perhaps become defined in terms of the Romans' Antonine Wall. We might perhaps be better trying to understand the situation by thinking of the Gap of Stirling and its strategic importance. Control of the Gap of Stirling has always been strategically important and we know there was trade from Scotland to Rome in skins and Caledonian bears, and might coal even have been mined along the shores of the Forth? Such goods as were obtained through trade with the country north of the Antonine Wall could well have been going out by ship from the Forth. Whoever controlled this gap could control the trade to some extent. This would make local fortified sites highly prized and the control of them a subject of ongoing dispute within peoples whose natural propensity was towards battle anyway. Add in the stresses of a struggle between two religions and we can see how a whole series of battles might occur here – just as they did in later more national and dynastic situations.

If indeed the Miathi were pagan when Aedan fought with them, then his son Artair can certainly be seen fighting in the right area against some of the right enemy to conform to my contention regarding the original Arthur. Most histories of Scotland, and Britain, say little of exactly how Christianity became the accepted religion and it has been suggested in some quarters that the people of Britain in the first to sixth centuries AD saw Christianity as being parallel to their supposed Druidic-based beliefs and were happy to accept the new faith. This type of thinking was particularly popular amongst those keen to differentiate the post-Reformation Presbyterian religion of Scotland from any association with Catholicism. By this way of thinking the Columban church had in fact been the true precursor of the Presbyterian religion and the hiatus of a thousand years when the Church of Rome was in charge was really no more than a break in tradition! The idea of peaceable conversion is highly unlikely, particularly when we think that St Constantine, reputed founder of Govan, was himself said to have been martyred in Kintyre in the sixth century, and others like St Donnan on Eigg met a similar fate a little later. The raids by Vikings on churches and monasteries in the ninth century have always been presented as driven by a lust for gold, but here again religion might have had some role to play. This might have been no more than making these Christian foundations 'fair game' with the booty in gold and silver a decided added attraction.

Much of our picture of this period comes from *Life of St Columba* – Columba was certainly not averse to battle if it suited him as the instance of the Battle of Cul Drebne shows. The story of him having a magic battle with the Druid Briochan in Inverness might easily be a cover for a more standard type of battle. As all of the early documents we have were written by monks, it is not surprising that the changeover is presented as absolutely natural, even inevitable. Another problem we have in trying to understand those times is the scarcity of written records from Scotland itself. So we have to combine archaeology, external sources and indigenous traditions to try and build up a picture of long periods of Scotland's past. In Columba we have a figure certainly capable of organising the equivalent of the later crusades in sixth-century Scotland. And in Artair mac Aedan we have a candidate for someone falling in such a type of battle, strengthened by Adomnan's use of the term barbarians for the Miathi. This is quite clear in terms of a classical education and the idea that has been suggested that it might simply apply to non Gaelic speakers is unlikely given we now know that the Picts and Scots and Britons seem to have lived alongside each other for centuries before this time.

If the situation regarding the struggle was volatile in the early part of the sixth century, and we know that even earlier the Pelagian heresy had caused widespread trouble within British

Christianity, there is little reason to think things would be much different in Columba's day. Columba has long been considered Scotland's foremost saint – his relics were even carried in to battle with the national army – and if as I have been suggesting the Arthur of the sixth century was important because of his involvement in Christianity, there would seem to be no reason why he would not be associated with this major figure. What we do have in the way of source material from the period or even earlier is generally pretty supportive of the Christian religion, even when it is material like the stories of *The Mabinogion* and the poetry of Taliesin. Aneurin, the supposed composer of *The Gododdin*, is a somewhat different case and *The Gododdin* is not particularly Christian. However, it may be that the Men of the North retained a special place in Welsh tradition precisely because of the involvement of some of their number in the eventual triumph of Christianity.

If the suggestion of Adomnan's battle with the Miathi being the same as the Battle of Manu mentioned in the Irish annals is correct this would put it in the general area of the Gap of Stirling. It could even include the possibility of it being at Camlaan. The Welsh sources survived many miles away from Scotland and Adomnan like Columba was a Gaelic speaker and he might not have had access to the same traditions as existed amongst the P-Celtic-speaking tribes. Additionally he was writing a century after the fact. This could be used to explain why such a major battle as Camlaan, occurring extensively in the Welsh sources, was not known to him by this name. D. F. Carroll, in *Arturius*, directly identifies this Battle of Manu with the Battle of Camlaan in order to substantiate the necessary dates proving that Arturius was the original Artair. In this he seems unaware that this is the most likely place for any battle to happen in Scotland particularly in a time when there was considerable ongoing strife. The Welsh sources are all agreed that Arthur's principal foe at Camlaan was Modred yet there is no mention of a named enemy for either the battle with the Miathi or in the Irish references to the Battle of Manu.

If he was the son of Columba's ally Aedan and was, as Carroll suggests, crusading for Christ, why was this not mentioned in Adomnan's *Life of St Columba*? In the mention of the battle against the Miathi there is nothing said about this Artair other than that he is one of Aedan's sons, prophesied by Columba to die in battle. There is certainly nothing like the mention in *The Gododdin*. This might be because in *The Gododdin* the Arthur referred to is part of pagan tradition but the Arthur of Nennius is also clearly a notable warrior, and significantly a war leader. There are no mentions of Artair mac Aedan either as a great warrior or leader in any of the Irish sources. As I am convinced Arthur was fighting on behalf of Christianity this seems damning. What we know of Arthur comes mainly from Welsh sources and it is extremely unlikely that a warrior from among the Gaelic-speaking Scots of Dalriada would find fame and glory amongst the neighbouring P-Celtic-speaking tribes without being noticed to the same extent among his own people. We do, however, seem to have a situation where Artair fell in a victorious Christian battle against a pagan force, precisely as happened to Arthur at Camlaan. If the accepted dates for Aedan's battle with the Miathi are even close we are only a few years from the Battle of Arderydd, which was certainly fought between Christians and pagans, so the situation was not yet finally resolved.

I believe there is one particularly telling point against this identification of Artair mac Aedan with the original Arthur. In many parts of Scotland we have references to Arthur – in the tale at Meigle, in place names and in the traditions of him lying asleep under such hills as the Eildons or Dumbuck Hill near Dumbarton. There is not a corresponding body of traditional material in Gaelic, the language spoken by Aedan and his son Artair, the language of the Columban church and the language of the first king to rule the combined Scots and Picts in the ninth century, Kenneth MacAlpin. It is generally accepted that by the tenth century virtually all of Scotland was Gaelic-speaking. While this is probably an exaggeration there is no doubt that Gaelic was the dominant language for a considerable time. To accept Artair mac Aedan as the original warrior hero Arthur we not only have to overcome the problem of dates but explain why such a notable hero can survive in the traditions of people who spoke a different language, traditions which were effectively transplanted elsewhere due to population movements in subsequent times. The traditions that do survive in Scotland, in Meigle and elsewhere, are likely to have survived originally through the medium of Pictish, or in what Koch called Common Archaic Neo-Brittonic, a P-Celtic language. It is likely that this covered a range of dialectal variation even within what we now call Scotland. What we do have in Gaelic tells of some aspects of Arthurian tradition and some of it, like the story of Mac Iain Direach, possibly arose from some truly ancient common source. But none of the Gaelic tales speak directly, or in detail, of the story of Arthur we know so well from the Welsh sources.

Chapter Nine

Conclusions

MOST COMMENTATORS LOOKING AT Arthur have attempted to make sense of the sixth-century historical figure against a background of widespread invasion. Today we are aware that the undoubted changeover from a predominantly P-Celtic-speaking population to a Germanic-speaking one was in reality a lengthy process, probably lasting centuries. Given that most of the surviving material referring to this period other than Latin annals and histories such as that of Nennius was originally written in the Welsh language, the tendency has understandably been to place Arthur within the landscape of Wales and south-west England. However, as we have seen all these sources tell us is that the Arthurian material survived long enough in Wales to be written down, and there can be little doubt that the original tales were part of oral tradition within the P-Celtic-speaking community of Britain as a whole. I have stressed the fact that the patterns of behaviour we see in the early material belong more to a tribal society than to anything like later nation states. In *The Gododdin of Aneurin* (p. xviii) J. T. Koch writes of the standard approach to interpreting source material from the Dark Age period: 'The implicit assumption is that the struggles recollected in the poetry attributed to Neurin [Aneurin] and Taliesin must have involved mono-ethnic forces with nationalist objectives'. He goes on to stress the complexity of the situation and the extent of time over which the language shift took place and then refers to the idea of the 'King of the English', telling us: 'The concept itself would have been precocious in the 570s.' (ibid) This makes absolute sense and obviously is as relevant to the first half of the sixth century when the historical Arthur was active. The acceptance of the idea that Arthur was effectively a war-band leader has not stopped him being presented as in some way representing either a nation or some kind of state. As Koch points out, the idea of kingship was anachronistic in this period and so, as we have seen, is the idea that any of the language groups of the time would have seen themselves a single people. It seems clear from what we can tell that the situation in the early sixth century according to the Welsh material was a fluid and ever-changing one. While we can be certain that the people living in Wales were still tribal we do not have a history of struggle there like that in Scotland. After the siege of Anglesey, Wales does not figure much in Roman accounts. However, as we have seen, Roman rule was subjected to repeated attack by alliances between people from different language groups from the north. The building of both the Antonine Wall and Hadrian's Wall clearly shows that the situation in the south of what we now call Scotland was extremely volatile from the first century AD onwards. From a very early period we are told that the barbarian alliances coming south included P- and Q-Celtic and Germanic-speaking peoples, all of whom I suggest were effectively tribal. We know that the tribes of Britain were capable of forming alliances for short-term purposes and we have to recognise that this includes Anglian speakers, either from tribes settled in Scotland or coming over from the Continent by boat.

In this respect we should perhaps look again at Bede when he talks of the languages of Britain. It has always been assumed that each of the language groups he mentions were living in distinct territories. The barbarian invasions suggest the situation may have been more complicated. Trying to delineate the exact territories of any of the Dark Age peoples seems essentially impossible. The suggestion that the area around the Gap of Stirling was one of mixed cultures and tribes would make sense in that this seems to have been an area which was often the location for battles. Given that battle was endemic amongst the warrior tribes of Scotland, this might in fact mean that the battles we do hear of were particularly notable. Such notable battles might not involve great numbers and certainly nothing like the vast armies that Geoffrey of Monmouth wrote of. The border areas between different tribes and groups of language-speakers might easily have been indistinct. Local traditions, like that of Taliesin having been born at Strathblane, support the notion of the Campsie and Kilsyth Hills being the northern limit of Strathclyde.

Where would such a border have run in the area adjoining the shore of Loch Lomond? This would seem to be an area where Britons and Picts and possibly even Scots would have been living alongside each other. The lands of Manau Gododdin might have covered both banks of the Forth, east of Stirling, again suggesting a situation that was anything but rigid, as might the fact that the Pentland Hills south of Edinburgh could contain a reference to Picts living in this area at some point. All of this surely serves to underline what we know from the Roman sources: that the peoples of these areas, no matter what languages they spoke, were capable of combining for a common purpose. Ptolemy's map from the second century describes what are essentially tribal groupings and there are no real reasons for seeing this as having fundamentally changed by the early years of the sixth century. These people lived in the same sort of subsistence economies, in small, widespread family groups, and were effectively organised as warrior tribes.

The Battle Campaign

The battles of Nennius are clearly part of a concerted campaign, whether or not they were in the order he gives or one of the alternatives I have suggested. What can hardly be doubted is that Arthur had a clear strategic aim in mind. We have seen that the idea behind most earlier interpretations of Arthur – that he was in fact leading resistance to invading forces from outside Britain – is unsustainable in the light of modern knowledge. If this was not the reason for the 'kings' of Nennius rallying behind a war leader, what reason can we suggest? We know the Caledonian tribes earlier banded together to resist Roman invasion so any reason for such a coming together would have to be significant. The answer to this seems to lie in the constant references to Arthur's Christianity. We know from St Patrick that the Picts were supposed to have reverted to paganism, though it is likely that only a part of them had even been Christianised in the first place. As I have shown, the locations of the battles given by Nennius can all be seen as being close to places that can be seen as being of pagan significance. Such sites could easily have been fulfilling similar functions amongst the different language groups as the pagan religion does seem to have been highly localised. This does not mean there would not have been sites that were important to people over considerable distances, as some of the major mountain sites and the Corryvreckan whirlpool appear to have been. What it does mean is that there does not seem to have been a centralised, organised and hierarchical structure akin to the Christian church, even if some particular locations might even have been the subject of pilgrimage in some form. The religious beliefs of such peoples are tied up with their ideas of family, ancestors and territory in ways that are difficult to see clearly from a modern perspective. I have suggested the existence of specific priestess groups in particular locations but it is notable that these locations were within the territories of people whom we see as essentially separate, for example Edinburgh among the Gododdin, Dumbarton among the Britons, Abernethy among the Picts and Kildare amongst the Scots in Ireland. Each of these locations I believe would be a focal point amongst the immediate tribe or tribal confederation of the area. I have found no evidence to suggest that these priestess groups were linked to one another or to some sort of hierarchic structure. They seem to have existed primarily within their own tribal grouping. However, as we know the tribes were capable of forming occasional alliances we can perhaps assume that there was some sort of commonality of belief and practice.

River Locations

In *Arthur and the Lost Kingdoms* (p. 210) Alistair Moffat draws attention to the fact that the locations by rivers would provide flat lands suitable for cavalry battles. This has something to commend it but we should remember that one of the most famous battles in Scottish history, the Battle of the Inch in Perth in 1396, was fought on foot on an island in the River Tay. This was fought between a selected number of men from two warring clans, or tribes, in a very formal fashion. Given what we know of clan warfare it is feasible that the choice of a suitable battleground could well have been the norm in earlier tribal society. The choice of a battle site is always of tactical importance and it is notable that several of the sites suggested are close to the sites of Roman forts. This suggests that the Romans found such locations to be of strategic importance. This could be because the pagan locations I have proposed were the natural focus for communal activities within individual tribal areas. The gathering of the men of the tribe for battle would naturally happen close to such locations. From the Romans' point of view the subjection of the natives would be enhanced if it could be accompanied by the destruction, or the acquisition, of politically important sites. As we have seen, the fact that a site has political and military importance does not rule out sacred significance, particularly within societies lacking the Chritian insistence on the difference between the sacred and the profane. Early kingship is always considered to have had some sacral importance and how much more would this have been the case in the role of chief within a pagan tribal society? The combination of sacral and political aspects of the chieftainship would tend to see them located in or close to such centres, the natural focus for tribe-wide communal activity. This means from a military–political viewpoint that these would be prime targets – for the Romans as a means of conquest or subjugation and for Arthur in terms of making his Christian victory as obvious as possible to the entire population of the immediate area.

Arthur and the Pax Romana

Many writers have seen Arthur as in some way as attempting to restore the sense of order that had existed under the Pax Romana. Given the suggestions for the battles given here this seems to me to be unsustainable. This interpretation seems to be to be more of a hangover from the classical education models of past education that anything based on a sustainable analysis of the material we have. In Scottish terms we have seen that the idea of client tribes is hardly sustained by the archaeological record. The Antonine Wall was occupied from when it was built in the early 140s AD until about ten years later. It was occupied again in the period 160–200 AD but we should remember that in this period Hadrian's Wall to the south was overrun by the combined forces of the barbarians, corresponding to the later alliances of the Picts, Saxons and Scots, in the early 180s AD. In the early years of the third century the Roman general Septimus Severus was actively fighting with the Caledonians and Maetae, and by 215 AD the Romans had retreated south to Hadrian's Wall which continued to be the northern frontier of Roman influence. The idea that in the short periods between 140 and 155, and 160 and 200 AD that the Pax Romana, the peace of Rome, could have been instituted over southern Scotland is frankly risible. Much of even southern Scotland is composed of high hills with deep winding glens and the inhabitants of the Borders and Galloway continued to cause problems to the governments of Scotland and England for hundreds of years. In Galloway the locals were not brought under effective crown control until the fifteenth century. The Border Reivers, like the Highland clans, were actively pursuing their own agendas until the seventeenth century. Yet there are those who still see the Romans as having pacified and controlled southern Scotland as they did England. The lines of Roman forts on the map of Scotland all follow strategic lines of communication and support. There is no real evidence for the growth of substantial native or Roman urban centres; the site at Camelon was built close to the end of the defensive structure of the Antonine Wall and can be seen as having a military function. Although there were substantial earth-built forts as far north as Fortingall in the Highlands and up the to the Pentland Firth there is no evidence for what we do see in England. There the Romans built substantial stone forts – and Hadrian's Wall, originally of turf, was eventually constructed entirely of stone. This never happened with the Antonine Wall.

Smyth makes the point in *Warlords and Holy Men* (pp. 40f.) that the number of Roman artefacts found in Scotland, though large, is much lower than for similar finds from East Prussia, an area that was far beyond the Roman frontier and was in fact never visited by the legions. While the Romans undoubtedly would have tried to secure alliances with what they considered frontier tribes, or hire them as scouts and so on, such behaviour would have been severely disrupted by the barbarian raids. There are even suggestions that some of the northern warriors working for the Romans turned against them. This would hardly be surprising as we know the tribes were loyal to themselves first and foremost and any relationship with the Romans would have arisen out of what they found convenient, rather than the other way round. Much has been made of the title Guledig that crops up in early Welsh sources. It has been suggested that this is an essentially Roman term and thus whoever had this title was seeking to re-impose something akin to Roman order. In fact the use of the term could easily have arisen from Latin literary practice. We rely on Christian scribes for the earliest literary sources and they in turn interpreted reality according to how they had been educated. This situation has been further complicated by the fact that Nennius referred to Aurelius Ambrosius as being of a Roman family, but says nothing of any relationship between him and Arthur.

This picture of a breakdown of civilisation and order with a consequent influx of barbarians taking advantage of the removal of Roman control to loot and pillage and then to settle has been shown to be unsustainable, though in Scottish terms it never fitted. In Scotland in the sixth century we are faced with a situation which, as far as the limited records and archaeology can tell us, was not significantly different from what it had been before Julius Caesar began the period of Roman influence over the southern parts of the island. Yes, the Romans were in Scotland. Yes, they created many marching camps and forts. Yes, they raised the Antonine Wall. But they were never in residence for more than a couple of decades at a time and if one looks at their occupation sites they can virtually all be analysed as being along lines of supply to a series of military campaigns rather than an attempt at full-scale absorption into the Roman Empire. England saw the growth of major urban centres under the Romans and the creation of extensive road networks. Scotland did not. England saw its population pattern changing with the urban centres acting as focuses for the surrounding countryside – a process probably advanced by the settlement of retired Roman troops given grants of land. Scotland did not. England had Roman courts and laws set up. Scotland did not. The idea that there could be any wish to return to the ordered society of Roman rule in Scotland has no basis in fact.

St Patrick and St Ninian

Christianity can be seen in Scotland from the fifth century. The letter St Patrick wrote to Coroticus 'king' of Strathclyde shows the latter to have been a Christian and as Patrick died before the end of the fifth century we can see that Strathclyde, with its capital at Dumbarton, was at least partially Christianised by the time of Arthur. Around the turn of the sixth century we have St Ninian active at Candida Casa, at what is now Whithorn on the Solway Firth. He is said to have had a successful mission among the southern Picts, which most would see as being beyond the Forth–Clyde line. So there is a strong possibility that Arthur could have been raised as a Christian, and quite probably in Strathclyde. At this stage, though Christianity was flourishing in parts of southern Scotland the population was still living in tribal groupings. Arthur would then have been brought up as a Christian within a warrior tribal society. We have seen that the tribes would need some overarching reason to band together and in this instance I suggest that the reason was to spread the Christian religion. Arthur appears to have brought the tribes together in traditional fashion in order to institute what became a revolutionary change in the tribes themselves. The institution of Christianity was something new. We know that Roman practice in pre-Christian times was usually to absorb local gods into the pantheon of Roman paganism, showing a form of religious tolerance that would make the absorption of new peoples into the ambit of Rome that much easier. Despite the re-use of pagan temples and other locations, the adherence to Christianity would provide a constant focus of loyalty outside the tribe. In time this would result in a weakening of the ties of loyalty within contemporary tribal society, changing the focus of inter-tribal relationships at the same time. This is unlike the situation at Mons Graupius where the confederation of tribes lasted only as long as was necessary. We should remember that we only have one account of this battle, and it is that Roman account that tells us they were victorious. It is in this weakening of the tribal ties and the consequent importance of the Christian church that we can perhaps see the trigger for the gradual move away from pure tribalism towards the creation of the nation state. And such nation states, complete with kings and centralised courts, would have Christian clerics in constant attendance. Such courts were centralised in function but not necessarily in locale, for even when Scotland as a whole became a nation it was customary for many generations that the court would travel around the country. Previous to the establishment of the monasteries there would have been no cohesive organisation within the pagan religion that could serve as a counterbalance to tribal interests. We can see something of the same process a couple of generations after Arthur's death with Columba manipulating the tribal system in Dalriada towards something more like a modern nation state, to further the Christian cause and his own interest.

Roman Cavalry Model?

That Arthur in Scotland had a troop of 300 professional warrior horsemen modelled on Roman practice as suggested by Alistair Moffat raises several questions. We know now that the idea of the concerted Anglo-Saxon invasion is untenable, so what would have been the reason for creating such a force and how could it have been sustained in an economy which as far as we can tell was dependent on basic self-sufficient arable and pastoral farming? The much vaunted notion of the superior warrior classes being supported by hard-working peasants is a feudal notion and what we know of ongoing tribal practice, in the Highland clans or the Border and Galloway kinship groups, suggests something completely different. The story told by Burt about the Highland clan chief in the 1730s and Martin Martin's comment that the

Highland warrior would follow a chief only if he liked him both speak of a situation where effectively all the men of the tribe were warriors, as well as farmers and stockmen. The organisation of a professional body of soldiers would be alien to tribal mores. I would suggest that Arthur did bring together a confederation of tribes for the length of his campaign (and we do not know whether the battles were fought in one season or several) but then the force disbanded. By the end of that campaign the main centres of religious practice had been Christianised, or had at least stopped being the focus of local pagan activity. Camlaan in this respect can perhaps be understood as the outcome of a later resurgence of anti-Christian paganism, an interpretation that could also apply to the later battle between Aedan Mac Gabhran and the Miathi 'barbarians'.

The finding of Roman silver or coins at places like Traprain Law has been used to argue for some kind of client relationship between the Romans and the local tribe the Votadini, whom we know as the Gododdin. A much more likely scenario is that this was loot or perhaps even the outcome of trading. After all, we have many references to raids on both the Roman Walls and no-one has argued for a money economy as early as this in Scotland. Nennius tells us of Ambrosius Aurelianus whom he says was of Roman descent but this was more than a generation before Arthur comes on the scene. The idea that Arthur was the heir to Roman ideas dies not hold up.

Kinship or Kingship?

All of those who have understood Arthur as having been primarily based in Scotland seem to have been confused by the idea of kingship. As we have seen, the key to understanding the period is kinship not kingship. Markale in *King of the Celts: Arthurian Legends and Celtic Tradition* (p. 114) describes the the basic social structure thus:

Tuath was a community formed by several *derbfhine*, or family groups. The *derbfhine* was the basic unit of Celtic society and consisted of four generations within one family, that is all the descendants of a single great grandfather. The egalitarian structure of the *fhine*, in which all wealth was owned collectively by the community, dictated the pattern of all social systems in Britain and Ireland.

He also makes the point:

The advent of conflict or war necessitated the election of a reg-s (Latin, rex) to take over responsibility for the defence of the community. The reg-s, literally the man who pointed the way, was elected from among his peers . . . His office was purely temporary and lasted only as long as the special circumstances which had made his election necessary in the first place. (ibid p. 115)

This explains the role of Arthur as a war leader. The tribal warriors understood battle, they understood loot, but it is debatable if they understood the concept of war other than as a necessity for resisting invasion. The attacks on the Roman Walls were certainly organised but they all seem to have been one-offs and not part of a cohesive political or military strategy. Given the make-up of the barbarian forces this is not surprising. In sixth-century Scotland there would have to have been something substantial happening to make Arthur's activities stand out. We know that inter-tribal warfare was endemic – the Highland Cateran tradition suggests a very structured approach to raiding and battle – and we also know that there had been co-existence between different language groups, the Scots of Dalriada providing some of the Pictish kings being a clear case in point. Germanic-speaking warriors were regularly joining the Celtic-speaking northern tribes in attacking the Romans. This fact raises some interesting questions: how did they arrive, where did they arrive, how closely linked were they to the tribes in whose territory they landed? This latter question is of fundamental importance. From anthropological studies of tribalism around the world it is apparent that in situations where tribes are regularly forming alliances, such alliances are often strengthened by intermarriage. Was this happening between the Germanic- and Celtic-speaking peoples whom the Romans tell us were regular allies? Whether such questions can ever be answered is a moot point but it is safe to say that any attempt to see Scotland at this time as organised along strict ethnic, linguistic or national lines is an exercise in futility. Arthur, however, does seem to have had an organisational structure in mind – that of the Christian religion

Mythical or Historical Hero?

Behind this historical Arthur leading the fight against paganism it is possible to see another shadowy figure. Many writers have commented that in his presentation within Welsh tradition he has some of the aspects of a god figure. The magical battles with giants, his similarity to Bran, the repeated occurrence of powerful pagan motifs such as the life-giving cauldrons and shape-changing maidens in various tales, and the adventures into the Underworld all speak of a figure arising from a mythological background. Within a tribal warrior society it would hardly be surprising to find a major warrior figure within the mythic and legendary corpus of traditional material. As we have seen, the distinction between historical and mythological figures in societies dependent on oral transmission need not be absolute. In effect, the transmission of cultural and educational material through oral transmission would tend to blur such distinctions. We know of many figures from both Irish and Welsh sources that are presented as gods but we do not know of them as the focus of anything we can identify as specific religious ritual. We know of such figures, including Arthur, being associated with prehistoric monuments such as cromlechs, chambered cairns and stone circles which at the least shows an idea of a continuity of sanctity at specific locales. It does not, however, show us altars to specific gods or goddesses. I would suggest that the paganism of sixth-century northern Britain was much more akin to what we would see as nature worship with specific sacred sites but no formalised religion in the sense that we understand it in the modern world. Within such a world view this merging of mythic and historic individuals could occur in the general idea of the ancestors – those who had gone before.

The process of storytelling in such societies can be seen as an essentially dynamic one: while there is a necessity for the subject matter at the heart of the material to remain constant, in a practical sense it could be adjusted according to circumstance, effectively allowing the story to be cast anew at every telling. We know this type of process was used by traditional ballad singers up to the nineteenth century in Scotland. This clearly counteracts what we would see as the necessity for absolute accuracy and truth. This would not apply to material like genealogies which would be recited by rote. What we might be seeing is a society in which there is a known mythic warrior called Arthur, a warrior who takes his name to assist him in leading other warriors who likewise know of the mythic warrior. It is even feasible to see an instance of something similar in the naming of his son Artair by Aedan Mac Gabhran, who would certainly have heard of Arthur. It is even within the bounds of possibility that the original Arthur was born among the Scots. Aedan's wife is said to have been a British princess, and such intermarriage would not be improbable in the scenario I have suggested for sixth-century Scotland.

In sixth-century Scotland we have a considerable number of P-Celtic-speaking tribal peoples, we have a series of excellent locations for the battles of Nennius and I have suggested a socio-political reason for a concerted military campaign. Most scholars now accept that a considerable amount of early Welsh material originally came from among the peoples of Strathclyde and Manau Gododdin, material I have suggested they would have shared with the Picts. In one sense Arthur is as much Welsh as he is Scottish –

the Welsh tribes believed that he existed within their environment as surely as we can see the P-Celtic-speaking tribespeople of the north did. In another sense Arthur is truly universal. He continues to inspire people throughout the world, as he has done for a millennium. His time and location depend on the sources we have looked at and I suggest the material can be better matched in Scotland than elsewhere. The socio-political situation in Scotland makes the idea of a concerted campaign highly likely. For those who see Arthur as having been the son of Aedan Mac Gabhran there are two problems I consider insurmountable. Most of the material that tells of Arthur survived in the traditions of the P-Celtic-speaking peoples, whether from Strathclyde, Manau Gododdin, Pictland or Wales. Given the location of the battles and the importance accorded Arthur in Welsh tradition, why is this not matched in Gaelic tradition? Yes, there are tantalising glimpses of some of the aspects of Arthur's story in tales like that of Mac Iain Direach but nothing that in any way resembles the detail and precision of the Mabinogion tales or the poetry of Taliesin. We know that Christianity triumphed in Scotland and Arthur was a Christian hero, so why does Adomnan tell us nothing more of Artair mac Aedan? The other point is the Battle of Camlaan. We have a date for this that is generally accepted by historians as 537 or 539 AD and the number of references to it in Welsh tradition underlines its importance. And this is where and when we are told Arthur died. Artair mac Aedan died in a battle with the Miathi, probably Picts, but we have no definite location or date for this. We do have a battle in the right period where we see a confederation of Christian chiefs fighting the pagan Gwendolau – Arderydd in 573 AD. I have heard it suggested that there has been a deliberate distortion of the sixth-century material to move Arthur back in history and thus hide his identity. We rely for annals and all early sources on Christian monks. Why would they deny one of their own?

As the stories of Arthur at Meigle, the Eildon Hills, even Arthur's Seat show, the story of Arthur has never been totally forgotten in Scotland. Storytelling carries on even after literacy arrives and the story of Arthur will go on and on. His actual location is probably less important than the fact of this continued existence, but in sixth-century Scotland we have the right places, the right background and the right traditions to say that Arthur, as a historical figure, fought his battles here. The mythic hero, perhaps still waiting in Avalon for the call to action, comes from even earlier in the human story, and who knows where or when he arose?

Nennius's Description of the Battles of Arthur

THE INTERPRETATION OF THE Battles of Arthur as presented by the eighth-century cleric Nennius, is included here as translated by John Morris. The suggestion that Nennius came across these battles originally in a poem, based on the possible rhyme scheme provided by the names of the battles, would support the contention in this book that they were fought as part of a concerted campaign, but not necessarily in the order Nennius states. The original was in Latin but contained obvious P-Celtic placenames.

> The first battle was at the mouth of the river called Glein. The second, the third, the fourth and the fifth were on another river, called the Douglas, which is in the country of Lindsey. The sixth battle was on the river called Bassas. The seventh battle was in Celyddon Forest, that is the Battle of Celyddon Coed. The eighth battle was in Guinnion Fort, and in it Arthur carried the image of the holy Mary, the everlasting Virgin, on his shield, and the heathen were put to flight on that day, and there was a great slaughter upon them, through the power of Our Lord Jesus Christ and the power of the holy Virgin Mary, his mother. The ninth battle was fought in the City of the Legions. The tenth battle was fought on the bank of the river called Tryfrwyd. The eleventh battle was on the hill called Agned. The twelfth battle was on Badon Hill and in it nine hundred and sixty men fell in one day, from a single charge of Arthur's, and no one laid them low save he alone, and he was victorious in all his campaigns. (p. 35)

While the Christian tone of this excerpt is obvious, the reference to Arthur laying low nine hundred and sixty men by himself seems to refer more to a mythological idealised hero than an actual physical person.

As with all material relating to the sixth century there will continue to be arguments as to the relevance and accuracy of material that only survives in later copies, but these battles have been used as the basis for trying to locate the historical Arthur over a considerable period.

Bibliography

Adomnan, *Life of St Columba*, tr. R. Sharpe (Penguin, London, 1995)

Aikman, J., (ed.) *The History of Scotland*, translated from the Latin of George Buchanan (Glasgow, 1827)

Alcock, L., *Arthur's Britain* (Pelican, London, 1971)

Anderson, A. O., *Early Sources of Scottish History* (Paul Watkins, Stamford, 1990)

Bede, *A History of the English Church and Peoples*, tr. L. Sherley-Price (London, Penguin, 1955)

Bellenden, J., *Translation of Boece's Chronicles of Scotland*, ed. W. Seton, R. W. Chambers, E. C. Batho (Scottish Text Society, Edinburgh, 1938)

Bower, W., *Scotichronicon*, ed. D. E. R. Watt (Aberdeen University Press, 1989)

Bromwich, R., *Trioedd Ynys Pridein: The Welsh Triads* (University of Wales Press)

Buchanan, George (see Aikman, J.)

Burt, E., *Burt's Letters from the North of Scotland* (John Donald, Edinburgh, 1974)

Campbell, J. F., *Popular Tales of the West Highlands* (Birlinn, Edinburgh, 1994)

Carroll, D. F., *Arturius: A Quest for Camelot* (D. F. Carroll, Coxhill, 1996)

Chadwick, N., *The British Heroic Age* (University of Wales Press, 1976)

Chadwick, N. 'Lost Literature of Celtic Scotland', *Scottish Gaelic Studies*, 7 (1953)

Cunliffe, B., *Facing the Ocean* (Oxford University Press, 2001)

Darrah, J., *Paganism in Arthurian Romance* (Boydell, Woodbridge, 1994)

Drummond, P., *Scottish Hill and Mountain Names*, (Scottish Mountaineering Trust, Glasgow, 1991)

Geoffrey of Monmouth, 'Vita Merlini (The Life of Merlin)', ed. J. Parry in *University of Illinios Studies in Language and Literature*, 10 (1925)

Geoffrey of Monmouth, *The History of the Kings of Britain*, tr. L. Thorpe (Penguin, London, 1966)

Gildas, *The Ruin of Britain*, ed. M. Winterbottom (Phillimore, London, 1978)

Gimbutas, M., *The Goddesses and Gods of Ancient Europe* (Thames & Hudson, London, 1996)

Glen, J., *History of the Town and Castle of Dumbarton* (Dumbarton, 1847)

Glennie, J. S., *Arthurian Localities in Scotland* (Llanerch, 1994)

Gluckman, M., *Politics, Law and Ritual in Tribal Society* (Blackwell, Oxford, 1971)

Gowans, L., 'Arthurian Survivals in Scottish Gaelic' in *The Arthurian Yearbook 2*, ed. K. Busby (Garland Publishing, New York & London, 1992)

Grant, J., *Old and New Edinburgh* (Black, London, 1880)

Graves, R., *The White Goddess* (Faber & Faber, London, 1961)

Hope, A. D., *A Midsummer Eve's Dream* (Oliver & Boyd, Edinburgh, 1971)

Howlett, H., *Highland Constable* (Edinburgh, 1950)

Hutton, R., *Pagan Religion of the Ancient British Isles* (Blackwell, Oxford, 1991)

James, S., *The Atlantic Celts* (British Museum Press, 1999)

Jervise, A., *The Land of the Lindsays* (Edmonston & Douglas, Edinburgh, 1887)

Joceline's *Life of Kentigern* in Scottish Hostporians (V)

Jones, G. & Jones, T., *The Mabinogion* (Everyman, London, 1993)

Koch, J. T., *The Gododdin of Aneurin* (University of Wales Press, 1997)

Loomis, R. S., 'Scotland and the Arthurian Legend' in *Proceedings of the Society of Antiquaries of Scotland*, lxxix (1955–9), pp. 1–21

Loomis, R. S., *Celtic Myth and Arthurian Romance* (Constable, 1995)

Macfarlane, W., *Geographical Collections Relating to Scotland*, ed. A. Mitchell, (Scottish History Society, Edinburgh, 1906–8)

Mackay, J. G., 'The Deer Cult and the Deer-Goddess Cult of the Ancient Caledonians', *Folklore*, no. 51 (1934)

Mackenzie, D. A., *Scottish Folk Lore and Folk Life* (Edinburgh, 1935)

Mackenzie, W. C., *Scottish Placenames* (Kegan Paul, London, 1931)

MacPhail, I. M. M., *Dumbarton Castle* (John Donald, Edinburgh, 1979)

MacQueen, J., *St Nynia* (Polygon, Edinburgh, 1990)

McHardy, S., *The Quest for the Nine Maidens*, (Luath Press, Edinburgh, Edinburgh, 2002)

McKenzie, P., *Camelot's Frontier* (Linghirst Press, Morpeth, 1999)

Malory, T., *Le Morte d'Arthur*, ed. J. Cowen, 2 vols, (Penguin, London, 1969)

Markale, J., *King of the Celts: Arthurian Legends and Celtic Tradition*, tr. C. Hauch (Inner Traditions Rochester, Vermont, 1994)

Markale, J., *Women of the Celts* (Inner Traditions Rochester, Vermont, 1986)

Martin, M., *A Description of the Western Islands of Scotland circa 1695* (Birlinn, 1994)

Megaw, J. V. S. & Simpson, D. D. A., *An Introduction to British Prehistory* (Leicester University Press, 1979)

Moffat, A., *Arthur and the Lost Kingdoms* (Weidenfeld & Nicolson, London, 1999)

Morte Arthur, ed. M. M. Banks (Longmans, Green & Co, London, 1900)

Nelson, G., *Huchown of the Awle Ryale* (J. Maclehose, Glasgow, 1902)

Nennius and the Welsh Annals, tr. & ed. J. Morris (Phillimore, London, 1980)

Nennius, 'The History of Britain' in *Arthurian Period Sources*, ed. J. Morris (Phillimore, London, 1980)

New Companion to the Literature of Wales, ed. M. Stephens (University of Wales Press, 1998)

Phillips, G. & Keatman, M., *King Arthur: The True Story* (Arrow, 1992)

The Pictish Arts Society Journal (PAS, c/o Pictavia, Brechin Castle Centre, Brechin DD9 6RL)

Randall J., *Arthur and Merlin: The Tweeddale Connection* (Selkirk, 1987)

Rees, A. & Rees, B., *Celtic Heritage* (Thames & Hudson, 1990)

Rennie, J., *The Scottish People* (Hutchison, London, 1960)

Rolleston, T. W., *Celtic Myths and Legends* (Bracken Books, London, 1986)

Screeton, P., *Quicksilver Heritage* (Thorsons, Wellingborough, 1974)

Skene, W. F., *Arthur and the Britons in Scotland*, ed. Bryce (Llanerch, Lampeter, 1988)

Skene, W. F., *The Highlanders of Scotland* (Eneas Mackay, Stirling, 1902)

Smyth, A. P., *Warlords and Holy Men* (Arnold, 1984)

Snyder, C., *The World of King Arthur* (Thames & Hudson, London, 2000)

Spence, L., *The Magic Arts in Celtic Britain* (Constable, London, 1995)

Tacitus, *On Britain and Germany*, tr. H. Mattingly (Penguin, West Drayton, 1948)

Taliesin, *The Book of Taliesin*, ed. I. Williams, tr. R. Bromwich (Institute for Advanced Studies, Dublin, 1972)

Tolstoy, L., *The Quest for Merlin* (Little, Brown & Co, Boston, 1985)

Veitch, J., *History and Poetry of the Scottish Border* (J. Maclehose, Glasgow, 1878)

Watson, W. J., *Celtic Place Names in Scotland* (Birlinn, Edinburgh, 1983)

Index

Some other books published by LUATH PRESS

The Quest for the Nine Maidens
Stuart McHardy
ISBN 0 946487 66 9 HBK £16.99

When Arthur was conveyed to Avalon they were there. When Odin summoned warriors to Valhalla they were there. When the Greek god Apollo was worshipped on mountaintops they were there. When Brendan came to the Island of Women they were there. Cerridwen's cauldron of inspiration was tended by them and Peredur received his arms from them. They are found in Pictland, Wales, Ireland, Iceland, Gaul, Greece, Africa and possibly as far as field as South America and Oceania.

They are the Nine Maidens, pagan priestesses involved in the worship of the Mother Goddess. From Stone Age rituals to the 20th century, the Nine Maidens come in many forms. Muses, Maenads, valkyries and druidesses all associated with a single male. Weather - workers, shape - shifters, diviners and healers, the Nine Maidens are linked to the Old Religion over much of our planet. In this book Stuart McHardy has traced similar groups of Nine Maidens, throughout the ancient Celtic and Germanic world and far beyond, from Christian and pagan sources. In his search he begins to uncover one of the most ancient and widespread institutions of human society.

Scotland: Myth, Legend and Folklore
Stuart McHardy
ISBN 0 946487 69 3 PBK 7.99

Who were the people who built the megaliths?

What great warriors sleep beneath the Hollow Hills?

Were the early Scottish saints just pagans in disguise?

Was King Arthur really Scottish?

When was Nessie first sighted?

This is a book about Scotland drawn from hundreds, if not thousands of years of story-telling. From the oral traditions of the Scots, Gaelic and Norse speakers of the past, it presents a new picture of who the Scottish are and where they come from. The stories that McHardy recounts may be hilarious, tragic, heroic, frightening or just plain bizzare, but they all provide an insight into a unique tradition of myth, legend and folklore that has marked both the language and landscape of Scotland.

FICTION

The Bannockburn Years
William Scott
ISBN 0 946487 34 0 PBK £7.95

The Great Melnikov
Hugh MacLachlan
ISBN 0 946487 42 1 PBK £7.95

The Strange Case of R L Stevenson
Richard Woodhead
ISBN 0 946487 86 3 HBK £16.99

But n Ben A Go Go
Matthew Fitt
ISBN 1 84282 014 1 PBK £6.99

FOLKLORE

The Supernatural Highlands
Francis Thompson
ISBN 0 946487 31 6 PBK £8.99

Tall Tales from an Island
Peter Macnab
ISBN 0 946487 07 3 PBK £8.99

Tales from the North Coast
Alan Temperley
ISBN 0 946487 18 9 PBK £8.99

Highland Myths & Legends
George W Macpherson
ISBN 1 84282 003 6 PBK £5.00

ON THE TRAIL OF

On the Trail of William Wallace
David R. Ross
ISBN 0 946487 47 2 PBK £7.99

On the Trail of Robert the Bruce
David R. Ross
ISBN 0 946487 52 9 PBK £7.99

On the Trail of Mary Queen of Scots
J. Keith Cheetham
ISBN 0 946487 50 2 PBK £7.99

On the Trail of Bonnie Prince Charlie
David R. Ross
ISBN 0 946487 68 5 PBK £7.99

On the Trail of Robert Burns
John Cairney
ISBN 0 946487 51 0 PBK £7.99

On the Trail of Robert Service
GW Lockhart
ISBN 0 946487 24 3 PBK £7.99

On the Trail of John Muir
Cherry Good
ISBN 0 946487 62 6 PBK £7.99

On the Trail of The Pilgrim Fathers
J Keith Cheetham
ISBN 0 946487 83 9 PBK £7.99

On the Trail of Queen Victoria in the Highlands
Ian R. Mitchell
ISBN 0 946487 79 0 PBK £7.99

HISTORY

Reportage Scotland: History in the Making
Louise Yeoman
ISBN 0 946487 61 8 PBK £9.99

Blind Harry's Wallace
William Hamilton of Gilbertfield
introduced by Elspeth King
ISBN 0 946487 43 X HBK £15.00
ISBN 0 946487 33 2 PBK £8.99

SOCIAL HISTORY

Shale Voices
Alistair Findlay
foreword by Tam Dalyell MP
ISBN 0 946487 63 4 PBK £10.99
ISBN 0 946487 78 2 HBK £17.99

Crofting Years
Francis Thompson
ISBN 0 946487 06 5 PBK £6.95

A Word for Scotland
Jack Campbell
foreword by Magnus Magnusson
ISBN 0 946487 48 0 PBK £12.99

CURRENT ISSUES

Old Scotland New Scotland
Jeff Fallow
ISBN 0 946487 40 5 PBK £6.99

Notes from the North
incorporating a Brief History of the Scots
and the English
Emma Wood
ISBN 0 946487 46 4 PBK £8.99

Trident on Trial
the case for people's disarmament
Angie Zelter
ISBN 1 84282 004 4 PBK £9.99

Scotland - Land and Power
the agenda for land reform
Andy Wightman
foreword by Lesley Riddoch
ISBN 0 946487 70 7 PBK £5.00

Broomie Law
Cinders McLeod
ISBN 0 946487 99 5 PBK £4.00

TRAVEL & LEISURE

Edinburgh and Leith Pub Guide
Stuart McHardy
ISBN 0 946487 80 4 PBK £4.95

Pilgrims in the Rough: St Andrews beyond the 19th Hole
Michael Tobert
ISBN 0 946487 74 X PBK £7.99

Let's Explore Edinburgh Old Town
Anne Bruce English
ISBN 0 946487 98 7 PBK £4.99

NATURAL SCOTLAND

Wild Scotland: The essential guide to finding the best of natural Scotland
James McCarthy
Photography by Laurie Campbell
ISBN 0 946487 37 5 PBK £7.50

Scotland Land and People
An Inhabited Solitude
James McCarthy
ISBN 0 946487 57 X PBK £7.99

The Highland Geology Trail
John L Roberts
ISBN 0 946487 36 7 PBK £4.99

Rum: Nature's Island
Magnus Magnusson
ISBN 0 946487 32 4 PBK £7.95

Red Sky at Night
John Barrington
ISBN 0 946487 60 X PBK £8.99

Listen to the Trees
Don MacCaskill
ISBN 0 946487 65 0 PBK £9.99

Wildlife: Otters – On the Swirl of the Tide
Bridget MacCaskill
ISBN 0 946487 67 7 PBK £9.99

Wildlife: Foxes – The Blood is Wild
Bridget MacCaskill
ISBN 0 946487 71 5 PBK £9.99

BIOGRAPHY

Tobermory Teuchter: A first-hand account of life on Mull in the early years of the 20th century
Peter Macnab
ISBN 0 946487 41 3 PBK £7.99

Bare Feet and Tackety Boots
Archie Cameron
ISBN 0 946487 17 0 PBK £7.95

The Last Lighthouse
Sharma Kraustopf
ISBN 0 946487 96 0 PBK £7.99

SPORT

Over the Top with the Tartan Army (Active Service 1992-97)
Andrew McArthur
ISBN 0 946487 45 6 PBK £7.99

MUSIC AND DANCE

Highland Balls and Village Halls
GW Lockhart
ISBN 0 946487 12 X PBK £6.95

Fiddles & Folk
GW Lockhart
ISBN 0 946487 38 3 PBK £7.95

POETRY

Poems to be read aloud
Collected and with an introduction by Tom
Atkinson
ISBN 0 946487 00 6 PBK £5.00

Scots Poems to be read aloud
Collected and with an introduction by Stuart
McHardy
ISBN 0 946487 81 2 PBK £5.00

The Luath Burns Companion
John Cairney
ISBN 1 84282 000 1 PBK £10.00

Men & Beasts
Poems and Prose by Valerie Gillies
Photographs by Rebecca Marr
ISBN 0 946487 92 8 PBK £15.00

'Nothing but Heather!'
Gerry Cambridge
ISBN 0 946487 49 9 PBK £15.00

Luath Press Limited

committed to publishing well written books worth reading

LUATH PRESS takes its name from Robert Burns, whose little collie Luath (*Gael.*, swift or nimble) tripped up Jean Armour at a wedding and gave him the chance to speak to the woman who was to be his wife and the abiding love of his life. Burns called one of *The Twa Dogs* Luath after Cuchullin's hunting dog in *Ossian's Fingal*. Luath Press grew up in the heart of Burns country, and now resides a few steps up the road from Burns' first lodgings in Edinburgh's Royal Mile.

Luath offers you distinctive writing with a hint of unexpected pleasures.

Most UK and US bookshops either carry our books in stock or can order them for you. To order direct from us, please send a £sterling cheque, postal order, international money order or your credit card details (number, address of cardholder and expiry date) to us at the address below. Please add post and packing as follows: UK – £1.00 per delivery address; overseas surface mail – £2.50 per delivery address; overseas airmail – £3.50 for the first book to each delivery address, plus £1.00 for each additional book by airmail to the same address. If your order is a gift, we will happily enclose your card or message at no extra charge.

Luath Press Limited
543/2 Castlehill
The Royal Mile
Edinburgh EH1 2ND
Scotland
Telephone: 0131 225 4326 (24 hours)
Fax: 0131 225 4324
email: gavin.macdougall@luath.co.uk
Website: www.luath.co.uk